The Rikki-Tikki-Tavi Imperative

The Business of Knowing What You Know, Then Managing by Experience

David P. Farnsworth

AllenPearce
PUBLISHERS

Contents

Acknowledgements

This book is dedicated to my mentor whom I call Richard in the text. Early in my career he guided me through the process of formalizing what I discuss in these essays and toward success in many other aspects of my life. None of the names used in the book are the real names of those involved, but all the experiences are real. My thanks to those who were part of the experiences I describe in these tags, including those who I may not show in the best of light; I learned from you as well. Thanks also to the many who read all or parts of the book and discussed the tagging concept with me. They know who they are. Paul was my editor and a great help in many ways. Defects, however, are mine. Finally, thanks to my family; parents, siblings, wife, kids. They all allowed me to enjoy an incredibly rich life as an avid internationalist. Much of what I experienced and talk about here was learned and then used as I saw that our world, if we wish it so, can be incredibly large.

If you like this book, talk about it: tweet, face, blog. If you wish to contact me, I am farnsworth547@comcast.net.

INTRODUCTION

Toward Knowing What You Know

"This has all happened before, and it will all happen again. This time, however, it happened to . . ."

"Everything that needs to be said has already been said. But, since no one was listening, everything must be said again."

"There are only two or three human stories, and they go on repeating themselves as fiercely as if they had never happened before."

" It's déjà vu all over again."

Whether it's the first line of a Disney fairy tale adaptation (*Peter Pan*), the musings of a French cynic, (Andre Gide), a fundamental premise in the writings of an American romantic novelist (Willa Cather), or just Yankee manager Yogi Berra spouting his own weird form of wisdom, these all remind us that many of our experiences are neither new nor unique. Knowing that situations repeat, return, and reoccur is one thing. Knowing how to turn that fact into a powerful advantage in your career, your home life, and just about anywhere else is another. I'm going to tell you how to do that.

As an attorney, I learned to recognize and accept precedent, the concept that the law should apply in the same way to the same set of circumstances. I knew that my MBA friends had been taught by the case method, analyzing real problems to learn lessons from them. I had, however, never heard them refer to a case they had studied when they confronted a problem. Learning from precedent, from what had happened before, seemed to be lacking early in my career and later as a spouse, a parent, and in other roles. I often felt like I was constantly reinventing the wheel as life kept serving up the same problems or opportunities again and again. I would find myself looking back at a situation and saying, "If I had only known then what I know now . . ." but wisdom always seemed to arrive a day too late.

I've realized since that often I *did* know better, but I hadn't structured my knowledge or my problem-solving skills in a way that allowed me to effectively *apply* my prior experience, my "precedents." I named this book after one of my favorite "tags," (Tags are what you will learn about in this book.). The **Rikki-Tikki-Tavi Imperative** tag is about learning, about gaining experience. However, nailing the right response to a situation is often not simply an issue of whether we might eventually figure out how to solve a particular problem; it's about recognizing the problem for what it is and then accessing the applicable understanding, skills, and experience we already possess. **We need to know what we know.**

My "ah-ha moment" came while I was working with Richard, the mentor I've dedicated this book to. The divisions we were leading were being negatively affected by incessant complaining from the head of a third division. His complaints weren't justified, but they were hurting our operations. As we discussed this problem one day, Richard said, "Well, this is clearly a 'throw the dog a bone' one."

I gave him a puzzled look. He explained: If a dog is barking, look to see if there is a cause, and then remove the cause. However, if there is no particular cause, and the dog is barking because he loves the sound of his voice, you have a couple of choices. You can shoot or otherwise get rid of the dog, or you can distract it. In our case, we couldn't shoot the dog (our complaining colleague), so we needed to distract him. We came up with an appropriate bone and temporarily resolved the situation while we worked on longer-term solutions in relative peace.

In future discussions on situation management, Richard explained that he had learned as a young executive that many of the issues he confronted and problems he had to solve were very much the same (notice I said *very much* the same, not *the same*). As he disciplined himself to recognize recurring situations, analyze their cause, and reach a resolution, he gave each of these reoccurring situations a name, a "situation tag," that would bring to mind both a similar problem and approaches and solutions that had worked in the past. He credited much of his rise (and it was meteoric) through the ranks of corporate management to this self-taught and ingrained ability to recognize and then resolve recurring problems quickly and effectively.

As I watched him work and tried to develop this skill myself, I realized that I had actually been using situation tags for many years (the **Sergeant York Strategy** and **Rikki-Tikki-Tavi Imperative** tags I describe later are from my preteen years). However, at that time I had never made the effort to formalize and organize them systematically as he had, so they had never become the potent tool for me that they were for Richard. He inspired me to adopt the discipline, and off I went.

I soon joined him in having a reputation for being able to quickly identify, restate, and resolve increasingly complex issues faster and more effectively than those I worked with.

I use dozens of tags now, the importance and usefulness of each ebbing and flowing as situations arise in business, marriage, child-raising, politics, and community service, among other roles. I've included thirty in this book (including **The Chaos Disclaimer**, a universal rule to rule the rules) so you can see how the tagging process works and get a feel for developing your own. You will find many that describe issues you recognize—I've tried to choose ones that are fairly universal. However, your own experiences may lead you to apply a different metaphor or tag to a particular situation. That's as it should be. I did the same thing with several of the tags Richard shared with me.

Situation tagging is about learning what *you* know and putting that knowledge to work for you. It's a giant step into a future of knowing better, faster, and more completely what you know. Being there will allow you to stride forward with confidence toward each objective on your own path to success in your job, your family, your avocation—your life.

CHAPTER 1

The Rikki-Tikki-Tavi Imperative

As a boy, one of my favorite authors was Rudyard Kipling. I dreamed of traveling to the exotic places he described and having adventures like Kim. I was fascinated by his humanization of animals and how he created their characters based on their natures and talents. It's no real surprise that one of his stories provided my first consciously implemented situation tag.

Kipling's Rikki-Tikki-Tavi is a mongoose who saves his human "family" from the horrible Nag, a monstrous cobra. What stuck with me, however, was not his bravery or fighting skills but his motto, which became this tag's imperative: "Run and find out." Rikki succeeded because he knew better than others what was going on, who was planning what, and when things were supposed to happen. If he couldn't run and find out himself, he sent someone else to gather information for him.

I adopted this motto early and pursued it to such a degree that I was occasionally banned from the local library until I'd gotten a good dose of fresh air and human contact. I was fortunate to live in a family and cultural environment that encouraged education, and self-acquired knowledge in particular. I'm sure you've heard the aphorism "knowledge is power." Well, if that is the case, then *seeking* knowledge is the foundation of *future* power. My father, an English professor, tried to impress this point of view on his students. I remember from my earliest visits to his office seeing advertisements he had cut out of *Time* magazine—I think they were from an oil company. They simply stated, "Send me a man who reads."

As I reached my senior year of high school I realized that although I had learned a great deal at school, this was not really where I had been educated. My education had come at home through family discussions, in libraries where I devoured books, and in museums, concert halls, churches, mosques. I had learned history through my travels at Persepolis, on the Acropolis, and at Buckingham Palace. I had also been educated on the farms where I worked most summers, learning both to work hard and more about agrarian economics than I could ever have gleaned from any book. I had been led to "run and find out" at many levels.

The importance of this imperative was driven home to me one day by my friend and mentor Richard, the one who led me to formalize my own situation tagging. I was working for him at the time and had complained about not having information I needed to complete a project. He looked at me with an impatient grimace and said, "Never complain that you don't know how to do your job. Just learn what you need to know and get it done."

The situation I was confronting required meeting with Communist government officials and convincing them to make concessions on behalf of my client. My main concern was meeting objections they might raise about my client's operations. Following my friend's advice, I determined to learn everything I could about what they would know and think about those operations. It turned out that their position would be based on an obscure, inaccurate but public white paper. I tracked down a copy and prepared to answer every concern based on both the accurate and inaccurate information it contained. Sure enough, as I entered the meeting, each of the officials had a copy of that paper on the desk in front of him, and they proceeded to present their objections just as I had expected—and I proceeded to diffuse them. I was prepared.

Looking at my own children and their peers, and my still much younger grandchildren and their peers, I fear sometimes that this lust to learn has been lost, replaced in large part by a desire to be spoon-fed or, and this is even more dangerous, to be entertained.

Through working with a number of high-tech trade associations, I learned that one of the most serious problems contemporary companies confront is the lack of an adequately educated workforce. One association I was involved with recently examined the state educational system, and we were discouraged, to say the least, by what we saw. To my mind, the most serious problem was neither investment nor teaching ability, though these are critical. I worried more about the attitude we found at all levels: students, parents, teachers, and administrations. We live in a marvelously enlightened country that has adopted universal public education as a right. What I observed in this study was that this right is being interpreted not as a right to access, which it is, but as a right to results, which it is not. Every young American should have access to a well-funded, competently administered public education with competent, qualified teachers on the front lines. The results of that access, however, are conditional on the students' and parents' contributions and effort, on each participant's own desire and commitment to "run and find out," which, sadly, is too often lacking.

This point was humorously but tragically illustrated by an incident reported by a high school English teacher. A student's father made an appointment and began their meeting by saying, "You have a problem. I promised I would buy my son a car if he got all Bs or better, and you gave him a C-minus."

"What's the problem?" the teacher inquired.

"Well, I want to buy him a car, so you have to change his grade."

The teacher took out the student's file and showed the father his work. He had unquestionably earned, at best, a C-minus. The father was incensed.

"Couldn't you have taught him better than that? Why couldn't you have made him get at least a B?"

The teacher pointed out that most of the students in her class had earned a B or better and that his son had had every opportunity to be among them. The father left, furious that she had kept him from rewarding his son's apparent mediocrity.

On a more macro level, our study discovered that more than 50 percent of students entering the local open colleges and universities required remedial math. Part of the problem, it appeared, was that the local high schools required only three years of math between ninth and twelfth grade, and most students were not taking any math as seniors. This meant they had had no math for more than a year prior to entering college. We prepared a well-reasoned presentation pointing out that if high schoolers took one of the math credits in their senior year, the need for remedial math at state colleges and universities would decrease dramatically, netting great savings to the state. We suggested as a further nudge that those savings could be diverted back into the high schools. After discussion and due consideration, the thirteen members of the state board voted unanimously against our proposal. When we incredulously asked why, the response was, "That's not what parents want; they want the senior year of high school to be a great socialization experience, and math in the senior year would limit participation in electives such as…"

The "run and find out" compulsion comes, as do most of my tags, with some cautions. You can appear to be (or even become) a busybody, a know-it-all, or evolve into the person who never gets invited to play *Trivial Pursuit*. I suppose at worst, if knowledge is power, and power corrupts, then knowledge can corrupt. I have occasionally been warned off myself. I worked in a group led by a president and two senior VPs. As legal counsel to the group, I made it my business to know the business, feeling I could protect and advise only as I understood. One day one of the senior VPs asked me into his office. In a kind and noncritical way, he noted that recently the president had been seeking me out for information and advice more and more frequently, often before speaking to either of the VPs or my director-level peers on matters concerning their own departments. He told me my peers were beginning to refer to me as "the ghost vice president" and suggested I remind the president on occasion that he could go to the original source himself rather than seeing me as the company database.

In general, however, "run and find out" has stood me in good stead. For most of my career, I have worked in high-tech and Internet companies, where technology moves so fast that keeping up with what I needed to know to do my job was, indeed, a race to find out. Much of the satisfaction in my professional life has come from running this race. I wish this curse on my children and children's children—that they may always feel compelled to run and find out. They will see as they do that learning is life's best form of entertainment, and I promise them they will never be bored.

The **Rikki-Tikki-Tavi Imperative** Restatement: In any situation where more knowledge is required to effectively deal with that situation, make to "run and find out" the first task. Never simply muddle through or do less than an excellent job because of ignorance. Teach any who will listen that the first object of education should be to instill a lust for learning itself.

Tagging Tip: Of Files, Folders, and Memos: Use tags to organize your personal experience.

We spend a great deal of time and money organizing our time, tasks, communications, and work. Our calendars are detailed reminders of what we have to do or have done. Emails are reviewed and deleted or carefully placed in a folder. Paper correspondence, notes, and other documents get filed in labeled folders and drawers. I had one colleague who kept every email he had ever received, carefully organized in folders and, to his great relief, now indexed. Another has everything he has ever written in the last fifteen-plus years in a single database, every word indexed. We expend great effort and care to organize our professional, social, family, and creative worlds so we can find what want when we want it.

But what about the knowledge based on both education and experiences locked in the increasingly large and complex files of our brains? Situation tags are the labels on the folders not of my emails or filing cabinets, but of my life and some of the important things that life has taught me.

I don't attempt to tag every solution to every problem I encounter. Most of my tags are broader than that. They relate to questions; they're issue statements that, when accessed, pull from my mind layers of experience and learning that can be applied to finding answers and solutions. Tags are the labels on the file folders, not the headings on each memo or note. The contents of each folder are there inside that marvelous memory system you are organizing, waiting to be accessed once you give that folder a name so you can find it again at will, a personal "Googlization" of your life.

CHAPTER 2

The 360-Degree Temptation

Before Jim joined our company, this friend and former colleague had been a naval officer who had spent the last part of his service as the navigator on a cruiser. He told me that his captain had been a micromanager with one quirk in particular that had seriously affected Jim's life. The captain insisted that anytime, night or day, mid-ocean or elsewhere, the ship deviated from course more than one degree, the deviation must immediately be reported directly to the navigator. This meant that while serving under that captain, my friend rarely got an hour of uninterrupted sleep. Ships in high seas or heavy wind seldom stay exactly on course, and a single wave or trough might be enough to throw the ship a degree off course.

Being off course, of course, could be a serious matter. A vessel that sails a hundred miles while one degree off course will wind up far from where it ought to be. However, modern ships have sophisticated navigational equipment and autopilots. In the case of my colleague's ship, the course would be corrected before the navigation watch could reach the navigator to report the now-corrected and irrelevant degree of deviation.

The ultimate consequence of the captain's unreasonable requirement was, my friend told me, the **360-Degree Temptation**. In order to demonstrate the complete irrelevance of the captain's painfully strict position on position, the navigation watch and helmsman would conspire to see if they could sail the ship in a full circle without the captain noticing that they had varied course. Apparently, on relatively smooth seas in the dark of an overcast night with no land light in sight, sailing in a circle is hardly noticeable to anyone not watching the navigational instruments. Since the ship was on patrol and not part of a convoy, the crew accomplished their circuitous conspiracy several times without anyone who mattered noticing. Having myself had the rather common experience of circling an airport in cloudy conditions without a clue as to where we were in that circle, I have no reason to doubt Jim's claim.

Finding the line between policies and procedures that assure effective order, not to mention safety, and those that lead to mocking disobedience, can be challenging. My most compelling experiences on the far side of that line came during a period when I traveled frequently to what was still Communist controlled and mostly Soviet Eastern Europe and Russia. On one trip to Moscow, officials at the airport found a slight error in some paperwork relating to my visa (their fault, I assure you). I was allowed to enter the country but on the promise that I would correct the problem. When I told my Russian contact what I was required to do, he looked at me in amazement and laughed. "What you are proposing," he said, "would take you every waking moment for more than the three days you plan to be here." He designed a workaround.

Another situation arose from a common rule in Soviet-controlled Europe requiring each citizen to report every contact with a foreigner to the proper authority. At the suggestion of friends, I purchased a complete Russian wardrobe and wore it while there so that those I met with had "plausible deniability": "He looked Russian to me." (To maintain the appearance, I did have to avoid speaking; my Russian is miserable.) I was good enough at looking like a local that Muscovites even stopped me in the streets to ask for directions. In fact, my charade actually gave me more in common with the locals that just my clothes. Because of the authoritarian and ridiculous rules that governed the Soviet systems, most comrades had a double life: an "official-facing" life, where they appeared to obey all the rules, and a "real" life, in which they did what they needed to do to get along .

One of the most delightful though dangerous 360-degree responses I learned about on my visits East was in Romania. During the Communist period, every typewriter in Romanian was registered, and a sample matching a required format was typed on each machine and kept by the security service. This allowed the secret police to identify the source of any "subversive" document and trace it to the typewriter of origin and the registered owner. The skill of altering typefaces was in high demand, not just for authors of subversive documents but also for the pure delight of frustrating the architects of a sinisterly stupid rule.

Of course, you don't have to look to the rigidity of the military or paranoid dictatorships to find rules that are, in the minds of the "oppressed," meant to be broken. The Prohibition era in the United

States provides a great illustration. More recently, prohibitions or limitations on using social media during work hours have led to media addicts stealing away to restroom stalls and broom closets with their cell phones. After all, there are no good reasons for those rules, are there? (For those who agree heartily with the prior statement, note that a frequent form of identity theft results when an employee with access to financial information overcomes an employer's security systems by phoning credit card numbers to outside partners in crime.) Speed limits are another target for scofflaws. Most of us can remember an open stretch of highway just begging us to "see what she can do if we open her up." Rules invite rebellion, and rules that we feel are ridiculous almost demand it. Of course, we have to define *ridiculous* with caution. To a teenager every rule may seem absurd and made to be circumvented, disregarded, or brazenly defied.

The **360-Degree Temptation** tag also forces me to look at my own rule-making—and breaking. I must determine whether it is the rule, rather than the deviant, that should be broken, lest my crew—whether it be family members, coworkers in a volunteer organization, employees, or colleagues—turn the ship out of sheer devilry or frustration. This tag has led me in my own management style to judge progress based on purpose and result and not primarily on process.

On the "rule-breaking" side, the **360-Degree Temptation** tag requires me to ask how I am responding to the strictures of structure myself. I am as subject as anyone to the temptation presented by that broad, straight highway, and why, if there is no traffic in sight and not a single bump in the road, shouldn't I try for a hundred and twenty? How am I responding to bad rule making? Do I put on my Russian overcoat and blend in? Do I line up with a "yes sir" and wake up the navigator? Or do I do what I can in an orderly, or less orderly, way to change misguided rules?

The **360-Degree Temptation** Query: As you make rules, policies, procedures, and processes, are you inviting rebellion or even mutiny? As you become aware of apparent insubordination, are you willing to ask if your rule making, or that of the organization, hasn't gone a bit too far?

CHAPTER 3

The Causation Query

My first inclination was to simply call this the "why" tag and comment on it in a single sentence: If I know "what," and am managing to "what," but don't know the why of that what, I don't know squat. However, the importance of the matter is worth a few more words.

A case study used by Steve, an acquaintance teaching at a business school, illustrates the what/why problem. During his tenure as a CEO, one of his divisions had an employee he called Joe for purposes of the case study. Joe, though an important and valuable part of a working group, had a significant problem: he was frequently late for work. Since Joe was involved in a manufacturing process that required the presence of each member of the team, his tardiness affected the whole group. Fed up, Joe's manager finally gave him a last warning. If he were late one more time, he'd be fired. The very next morning Joe was late.

My friend stops the story here and asks his class each year whether, as Joe's manager, they would fire him or give him one more chance. By show of hands, each year the class is fairly evenly split. As Steve described this to me, however, his concern was that never had a single student stopped the discussion to get to the real crux of the exercise. At the point where he pauses for the vote, there is no way the students can make an appropriate decision because none of them knows *why* Joe was late the morning after the last warning. Was he simply continuing a habit of lazy thoughtlessness, or, on that day, did he stop to save a life? Did his car actually stall, or did the dog really eat his homework? These students, who were preparing to go forth as captains of industry, were making a critical decision without knowing squat.

"Why" is a hard taskmaster because it can arise in so many contexts. Often it relates to justification. One of the most common questions in life, particularly when we are young, is "What did you do that for?" a grammatically abominable way of asking, "Why did you do that?" with a strong "dimwit" or worse epithet implied if not actually spoken. Regardless of the grammar, the demand that someone justify him- or herself is a poor management tool when used primarily to convey condemnation.

"Why" can also raise the question of motivation. I worked for many years as counsel to an advertising group and watched its members spend millions upon millions of dollars in pursuit of the why. The issue of why in advertising has become so critical, particularly in the "Internet for free" context, that behavioral advertising is raising a crisis of privacy stemming from how willing we are to let others know the whys of our lives. Despite appearances, advertisers, who educate themselves by following our every action on the Internet, our cell phones, and everything we do in our virtual or real worlds, are not primarily concerned with *what* we do. They don't even care who we are. What they really want to know is why we did what we did so they can get us to do it again, or not do it again, or do something else. To them, motivation is everything.

Perhaps the ultimate why issue is causation. I recognize, of course, that causation is a sticky wicket; too often we believe that because two things are related, one caused the other. We are caught up in "evaluation by simultaneous presence" (see the **Dumpster Dilemma**) but may not really have any basis for the conclusions we draw.

In an organization I led for a number of years, I occasionally frightened the staff by having a single point on the staff meeting agenda: the word *why*. It made them nervous. In this meeting each member of my staff was not to tell the group primarily *what* they were doing, but *why* they were doing whatever. It made them nervous initially because they thought of it as a demand for justification. It wasn't; it was about causation, and they soon caught on. We were running a charity, and I wanted all of us to feel sure that we were still thinking and acting charitably and had not lost sight of the cause that had brought us together in the first place.

This brings us back to Joe. Was Joe late for a good why or a bad why? Justification. Did Joe stop to help someone out of the goodness of his heart? Motivation. How did Joe get caught up in whatever delayed him? Causation. I don't know the reasons behind Joe's tardiness problems, but I can relate in a small way to his predicament. I was on the executive committee of a community charity that met once each month early in the morning so that each of the important members could get on with his/her day. One bitter cold morning I arrived at the meeting very late. I walked in recognizing that I had upset the schedules of twelve other people who had plenty to do. Their frigid stares did melt to a degree when I explained that I had gone considerably out of my way to take a homeless man I had seen walking along the dark road to a shelter where he could spend the day. What I didn't add, and I doubt it came to anyone else's mind, was the question as to why I was the one that was late. I knew where each of the members of the committee lived, and at least half of them had to have passed that man on their way to the meeting.

I was born into a great, wonderful, loving family that supported me without question or compromise, but I have to confess that had I been able to think and speak on the day of my birth, my first word still would have been, "Why?" Perhaps it is that "accident of birth," if you will, that leaves me wanting to be sure I am involved in good things for good reasons and have the right answers for justification, motivation, and, the big why, causation.

The **Causation Query** Restatement: In any situation where you are asked to make a significant commitment of effort, time, or money, or to judge the efforts of others in those contexts, make sure to learn the why behind the efforts, not just the what.

Tagging Tip: "Even the Longest Journey Begins . . .." Use situation tags to get your thinking started in the right direction.

Those who recognize this quote, variously attributed to Lao-Tzu or Confucius and variously translated, would end it with ". . . a single step." That's true, of course, but I want to step back from that step and establish a more demanding requirement. Any journey, if you want it to be an efficient and effective one, begins with knowing where you are. In a new place when we open a map (or our smart phone) to get us where we want to go, our first question is, "Let's see, where are we?" When a lost friend calls for directions, we ask, "Where are you now?" Guidance requires a starting place.

I have traveled a great deal during my career, and in each city I visited I soon had a place or two that became reference points from which I felt comfortable branching out to explore. For example, standing in Piazza Barberini in Rome, I know that if I go up the hill one way, I get to my lawyer's office; the other, the U.S. consulate. To one side up an alley is my favorite restaurant in all of Italy. In the other direction are the Trevi Fountain and the Coliseum. I don't know the names of all the little streets around me, but I have a firm grasp of where I am.   It's almost as nice as the comfort that comes when, returning from a long trip, I say, "There's Mona reservoir; I'm almost home."

Our physical lives are filled with places that provide the comfort of familiarity: landmarks and reference points. In the physical world we make it a point to know where we are. Why not become equally adept at mental mapping? This is a main object of situation tags. We can say, I recognize this place; I have been in this situation before and am prepared to take the next step. If every journey, physical or mental, place to place, or process to process, begins with a first step, knowing where we are allows us to make that step in the right direction.

CHAPTER 4

The Bastogne Response

In December 1944, as the Allies pushed through France and Belgium deeper into Hitler's Third Reich, the Germans launched a desperate counterattack that became known as the Battle of the Bulge. The Nazi armies pushed quickly back into France and Belgium, and the U.S. 101st Airborne Division, holding the town of Bastogne, Belgium, was surrounded and besieged by a much larger force. Bad weather made airdrops to resupply the Americans impossible, so the beleaguered troops were in a seriously bad way. Recognizing their distress, the German general sent the American general commanding the city a well-reasoned and rather gentlemanly demand that the U.S. garrison surrender. He pointed out that they were surrounded, they were out-gunned, they were sure to be defeated, and that continuing the battle would result in great loss of life to both soldiers and civilians. He pled for the U.S. general to contemplate the cost in humanitarian terms. The German note contains more than 170 words.

The American response was returned rather quickly and has become one of the most famous wartime communications of all time. It consisted of a single word: "Nuts." The American officer who delivered the message knew that the Germans would not grasp this American colloquialism and explained that in plain English it meant "Go to hell." Actually, since General McAuliffe, the American commander, had a reputation for never using profanity, the proper translation would be "Absolutely not; no justification to be provided."

The **Bastogne Response** is one of my most used tags, since I have become concerned that I may have lost the ability to say no in absolute terms. There are many reasons for reluctance to engage in absolute negatives (or absolute anythings, for that matter). We hope for a "teaching moment" to help someone come to understand our point of view. We don't want to offend, make others feel bad, or damage self-esteem. Being unconditional may appear politically incorrect. Sometimes we just aren't willing to accept the consequences of saying no and end up, instead, letting bad things happen or decision making become a drawn out stand-off, hoping that someone we should have given a simple no to will give up and go away. In those cases, our ambivalence and wishy-washiness wastes emotion, time, and money.

Of course there are times when "No" should be tempered with teaching; the "Why" behind the response will help the recipient learn how to approach an issue more successfully next time. Yet even in those cases, I have learned it is often more productive to save the teaching for later, when the disappointment of rejection has passed. No can also be said with an appropriate degree of kindness and gentility; being absolute does not mean being mean. General McAuliffe did not, in fact, say, "Go to hell!"

A memorable "No" moment came when I was engaged in a delicate government-relations effort. We were dealing with a literally very divided house, and it was completely unclear which side would eventually end up in power. At one point, a representative from one side approached us for a favor. Granting that favor would have strengthened our position if that side came to power, but damaged us if the other side won. I told the requestor we would take the issue under advisement and took the matter to my boss. He listened patiently, looked me in the eye, and said, "No, and you know better than to have asked."

He was right, I did know better, and so did the person who had asked the favor of me in the first place. Perhaps the most important use of the **Bastogne Response** is in situations where the request comes from someone who should have known better than to ask and is hoping that a higher authority will help justify a planned misdeed or questionable activity. Those who have raised children through their teenage years (or any years, for that matter) will certainly recognize this ploy.

The **Bastogne Response** brings with it a significant risk (or perhaps many risks, but this one bothers me the most): What if the asker simply will not take no for an answer? One of the great disappointments in my career came while helping a client negotiate an intellectual property license. I was given a draft of the agreement for review, parts of which had been written by the other party. This "other party" can only be described as a stubborn old codger, and he refused to use an attorney. His draft left much to be desired, but he insisted that his wording be used. I pointed out to my business group that his wording would leave important elements of the license ambiguous. I was unsure he even understood our intended use of the licensed property. I said bluntly that we should tell him no when it came to using his draft; we should make the agreement legally clear even if he didn't like it and be absolutely sure as a result that there was a mutual understanding as to the nature of the license. My audience didn't want to hear my no and felt that if we pushed for the clarity I wanted, the man would demand more money. They wanted instead to get confirmation that a judicial interpretation of the ambiguity would likely be in our favor. Our advising counsel confirmed that that would be the case.

As it turned out, the old codger did take umbrage at the way we used the material and interpreted the ambiguity the way he thought he wrote it. After years of wrangling, we ended up paying as much for the license as we would have had there been a clear, mutual understanding from the outset. That we may have been legally correct became irrelevant as other factors intervened.

The **Bastogne Response** exposes the fact that as a society we find it increasingly difficult to say no in any absolute sense, whatever the reason. We find it equally difficult to be told no; such absolutes offend our sense of individualism and our apparently fragile self-worth. Perhaps most unfortunate, moral boundaries are increasingly less likely to be seen as acceptable grounds for an absolute no.

One of my favorite management books is a short volume on negotiation called *Getting to Yes*. While its authors do note that there must be a line in the sand in every negotiation where a party simply says no and walks away, I think that point is worth further investigation. I think we could use an equally well-reasoned companion volume titled *Getting to No*.

The **Bastogne Response** Restatement: Never be afraid, when the situation requires, to say "No" and mean "Absolutely not," particularly when that answer is required as a moral imperative.

CHAPTER 5

On Darley's Law

(Note: This essay differs from most in the book. At the request of a member of a state Board of Education, I added solutions as well as defining the situation.)

A recent conversation with Sharon, a former colleague and now a professor of organizational behavior, turned in due course to performance-based reward systems and the often-stated principle, "That which is measured and rewarded is that which gets done." She described the performance-based reward history of an organization that she had recently left. They, as a service organization, had decided to reward each branch office based on the number of "success stories" resulting from services performed for their clients that the branch could report.

Shortly after this system was implemented, Sharon asked an employee in a branch office she was visiting what her job was. She replied, with only limited display of embarrassment, that she was the success story creator. Sharon later learned that many of the branch offices had created similar positions and that the definition of a "success story" was being rapidly and radically altered throughout the organization. A success story was no longer the result of meaningful service to a client, but merely whatever allowed an office to demonstrate a high degree of success. In one office, every client contact became a success story. This corruption soon destroyed all efforts to reward meaningfully measured behavior. The attention of employees and management was diverted to very creative, but mostly meaningless, activity.

Sharon then told me that the process of organizational corruption she had described had been studied and defined by a Princeton psychologist who became the source for the phenomenon's name: "Darley's Law." Simply put, Darley's Law states that "the more any quantitative performance measure is used to determine a group's or an individual's reward or punishment, the more subject it will be to corruption pressures and the more apt it will be to distort and corrupt the action patterns and thoughts of the group or individual it is intended to monitor."

Darley's Law has reared its head in everything from school districts falsifying test scores to assure federal funding to Wall Street executives creating fanciful forms of value to assure massive bonuses.

However, the likelihood of Darley's Law being a realistic expression of human nature aside, it does not mean that performance-based reward systems should be abandoned. Rather, it means that they should be carefully structured, closely monitored, and rigorously re-evaluated on a regular basis. A few simple principles operating together should allow most organizations to avoid running afoul of **Darley's Law**.

First, of course, quantitative measures must reflect the real objectives of an organization. If an organization is going to be distorted, it should at least distort toward real value. Too often objective standards are " feel good" or "flashy," not fundamental.

Second, multiple measures should be used to evaluate performance. This should be relatively easy, since good results from an individual or an organization are seldom the consequence of a single factor. Measuring performance against multiple factors makes it more difficult to game the system and create the appearance of success without achieving what really matters.

Third, the measurement tools must be as free from corruption or undue influence as the objectives to be measured. Just like multiple objectives, multiple tools thwart attempts to game the system.

Fourth, part of the system, for both objectives and measurement tools, should be qualitative and subjective, perhaps even arbitrary (*Discretionary* might be the best word). The evaluator must always have the right to declare foul and reward or punish accordingly.

Fifth, and this relates closely to the fourth principle, the "buck" must stop with a human being or, at worst, a small group of human beings. This individual or group must wield the discretionary sword. The manager must not be able, upon rewarding measured but nonproductive performance, to say, "Well, they met their numbers so I had no choice but to provide the reward."

Sixth, the person or group where the buck stops must be measured and rewarded based on criteria different from those used to reward those they are measuring. If management merit is evaluated in exactly the same way as that of those managed, the tendency toward corruption will be amplified, both because management wants to be rewarded itself and because subordinates will be motivated to corrupt the system not only for their own reward but also to please the boss and assure his or her own reward. To be sure, upper management should be rewarded based on the measured results applicable to the organization, but they should also meet additional criteria. Generally, they should be measured against not just whether an objective is met but also, and perhaps more importantly, on *how* an objective is met: no unnatural acts, no destruction of morale, no meeting a quantitative goal at the risk of qualitative destruction of future opportunity.

Avoiding or remediating the effects of **Darley's Law** in an organization with highly quantitative objectives may be difficult and certainly requires new and outside-the-box thinking. In organizations working toward performance-based rewards, it requires deciding that avoiding these effects is a mandatory, integral part of the measurement and rewards process. While overt action to steer clear of **Darley's Law** may appear as cynical mistrust of an organization and of the individuals working within it, I suggest that following these principles is a protection and shield to the integrity of both. I love and trust my grandchildren and train them to be honest, but if I don't want them to eat the cookies, I don't leave the cookies lying around.

The **Darley's Law** Restatement: When creating a system that rewards performance based on measured objectives, expect Darley's Law to influence the situation and take preventative action up front.

CHAPTER 6

Maryruth's Rule

My wife's name is Maryruth, one word, no cap on the *r*, as I have explained a thousand times when introducing her, especially to those perversely dedicated to spelling her name wrong on some form or another. Last time I Googled it, I found no other person with that apparently unimaginable spelling bequeathed her by a father trying to placate all the females living in a crowded home. This tag is named after, and arises from the priorities of, my wife of more than forty years.

As we became a couple, we received notices of events in the lives of friends or acquaintances of one or the other: wedding announcements, graduation announcements, notices that this or that relative was in a play, moving into a new home, or otherwise involved in some, to me, unimportant happening. The notices from and about relatives were more often from my side: I have over 100 first cousins, and this may be why I responded differently to those invitations. Often on receiving one, I would say something like, "Well, they sent me an invitation out of a sense of obligation; they really don't expect me to attend or respond." There it is, the key word in **Maryruth's Rule**: *expectation*. My soon-to-be-wife would respond, "David, our response to others shouldn't be based on their expectations; we want to respond in a way that they will be pleasantly surprised." Maryruth, as part of her very nature, when choosing a gift, responding to an invitation, or otherwise giving of time, talent, or effort, always goes beyond expectations to be sure that the recipient will be pleasantly surprised. Often, since the other person had no real expectation at all, the result goes well beyond mere pleasant surprise and even approaches amazement.

As I have tried to adopt **Maryruth's Rule**—and it has been difficult for me because it is not in my nature—I have noted how in almost every formal setting in which my behavior is evaluated, expectation has been the key. "Meets expectations, exceeds expectations, greatly exceeds expectations." These standards have always bemused me, in part because I was raised in an environment where the expectations were always so high that even meeting them was nigh impossible. Maybe the better evaluation form would read "In working with this individual, were you (check one) __sometimes, __frequently, __always pleasantly surprised at his/her contribution?"

There may be a downside to **Maryruth's Rule**. Unfortunately, Maryruth has never learned to say no, even when the request may deserve the **Bastogne Response.** My wife has more "best friends" than I have acquaintances and accumulates more just about any time she says "Hello." Move over you Facebook junkies; my wife has more "friends" than you can imagine, and they are real.

Maryruth's Rule Restatement: When dealing with anybody, don't stop at expectations. Make sure that every action leaves others pleasantly surprised.

Tagging Tip: Avoiding a Wild Goose Chase: Use tags that are meaningful to you rather than adopting common aphorisms.

We all already use analogies to describe common situations. In developing situation tagging you might be tempted to use common metaphors. For example, at the end of a futile effort to accomplish something, we complain that we have been on "a wild goose chase." Most of us, however, have never chased a wild goose. It is worth chasing that metaphor to clarify why using tags based on current clichés may not be that useful. Admit it, you have used "wild goose chase" frequently but really don't know what it means.

The phrase "wild goose chase" comes from a time when productive small-game hunting was done with falcons and hawks. Falcons and hawks are very effective at bringing down doves, pigeons, and other small birds, as well as larger birds that are not fast or long-distance flyers. A wild goose, however, is a very large, fast bird--faster over any significant distance than a falcon or hawk and large and strong enough that it would likely recover from a strike by a smaller bird. Sending a falcon after a wild goose is an exercise in futility. An experienced falconer will not release his bird to chase a wild goose and will call it back and punish it if it engages in that pursuit while supposedly after other game.

Using metaphoric epigrams to organize knowledge and experience may be just a wild goose chase if we simply adopt phrases that are not really meaningful to us.

The Second Opinion Requisite

With the pressures of job, family, politics, and social life now being coupled with the burden of near-constant information overload, life seems determined to force us to make decisions about increasingly complex matters under ever-shorter deadlines. Recent management books, particularly those written in connection with the early evolution of the Internet, try to teach us that if we can't act at the speed of light, we will be left behind; competitors will eat our lunch before we even get to the table. Noting that many of the companies developed under that philosophy died ignominiously when the Internet bubble burst, and having worked for more than twelve years for a successful one that didn't, I say with little humility, "Bull!" Sure, we have to act in a timely manner, but speed for its own sake takes us quickly down a slippery slope.

Based on the situation tag titling this section and my confessing right now a personal aversion to pressured decision making, you probably think I'm going to recommend that before you make any significant, complex decision or accept such decisions from others, you should consult with a second, informed source for confirmation or another point of view. While that is a wise choice, that is not the object of this tag. This tag arose from the following experience.

Some years ago I joined a company as their sole in-house counsel. Only a few months into my time there, we had the chance to make a significant acquisition, one that would change the very nature of the company. Being an underfunded startup, we decided to do most of the work on the acquisition internally; that is, I would do it. I did due diligence and prepared the documents very carefully, using guidance and checklists prepared by others with far more expertise. I finalized the documents one afternoon and went home satisfied that I could get a good night's sleep. Everything was well prepared for closing the transaction the next morning.

Far too early the next morning I woke with a start, convinced that I had not resolved two major points as I had finalized the documents. Rushing to the office, I grabbed the papers and, as I began to search through them, expressed my concerns to my paralegal. She gave me a questioning stare and assured me that the issues had been fully reviewed and resolved. As she recounted the process we had followed, I remembered that the issues had been raised by one of the checklists. I recognized, however, that checking something off a list and truly believing that I had applied my full mental faculties to an issue were two very different things. My "wisdom" mind had taken the more relaxed nighttime hours to catch up with a matter that had already been resolved by my "checklist" mind.

We can all think of similar, if less critical, experiences. How often have we packed for a trip against a checklist but doubt the next morning as we are about to leave that we really have everything. We remember twenty-four hours later the answer to a question that we missed on an exam or come up with a solution we wish we could now apply to a problem that we solved less elegantly yesterday.

I decided after some experience applying the **Second Opinion Requisite** that, in fact, it takes about twenty-four hours and sleep for my short-term memory (the checklist and cram-for-exam memory) to check in with and correlate information with my long-term memory. I was gratified to read recently that studies have confirmed my hypothesis. Confidence, and I believe wisdom, arise only when we allow our own brain to submit its "second opinion." Thus, the **Second Opinion Requisite** is not so much a matter of asking someone else for their opinion, but rather, at least as often as possible, letting the other half of my brain weigh in and contribute its point of view. In fact, it may be that for full wisdom to be brought to bear and for us to express our best selves, many parts of our mind and memory need to be consulted, and some of them seem to respond less quickly than others.

A good analogy is a webpage. Every webpage we view while browsing the Internet is made up of multiple frames. Each of those frames can be sent from a separate source, and the sources may be thousands of miles from each other, on separate servers. Each serving computer will likely operate at a different speed and have its own load (the number of demands made on it) to deal with. Fortunately, because most modern servers, computers, and connections operate at very fast speeds and transmit data to a webpage at close to the speed of light, a page with multiple frames will usually generate in such a way that we don't detect the distinct arrival of the separate frames. However, I am sure we have all experienced the situation where, because our computer is receiving strangely or the servers sending the separate frames are out of sync, a webpage falls together piece by piece. Although the difference in arrival times may be measured in milliseconds, it becomes noticeable. I know from many years at an Internet company that this "frame latency" drives web developers crazy.

Similarly, it may drive us crazy to realize that the various parts of memory, muscle training, and our ability to act and express don't all operate in the same manner or at the same speed. This is typically most true when we are under stress, when one part of our "framing system" may override others as our mind and body try to decide which elements get precedent. Unfortunately, it is in times of stress that the **Second Opinion Requisite** may be most critical. Our willingness to step back and confess that we need to "sleep on it" may make the difference between a "What's the matter? Do you only have half a brain?" decision and the wisdom that comes from having our full faculties involved.

The **Second Opinion Requisite** Restatement: In situations where circumstances allow, take enough time for decision making to become confident that you have applied your best wisdom to the matter, including "sleeping on it" when necessary, even—and especially—if you are driven by unrealistic restraints to act quickly.

CHAPTER 8

The Truckloads of Dirt Requirement

An ability that I have always considered one of my greatest gifts is being able to organize and manage the various parts of complex problems in my head, (partly, I suggest, because of the system I present in this book). As I began to work in the European office of a large global concern, I felt this ability to be particularly useful. I was counsel to a number of groups that needed to achieve common goals not only in coordination with each other but also with their headquarters' counterparts. I soon found myself in the middle of a number of large, complex projects and began to see myself as the chief organizer, the one who could see all the parts and hold the project together.

One day, after I had brought one of these projects to a successful conclusion well before the deadline and with better results than anyone had expected, I was called into the office of the division president. I went up to see him very pleased with myself and expecting to be showered with praise. Our meeting turned out quite differently from my expectations.

"Farnsworth," he said "you have just moved a mountain, and that is amazing." "However," he went on, "you need to understand that while you were running this project, I deflected an incredible amount of criticism away from you, and it wasn't just from people here; it was from headquarters, including your boss and mine." I was dumbfounded. I had just completed one of the most complex projects the group had ever dealt with, I had moved the proverbial mountain, and here I was being criticized!

My friend, protector, and eventual mentor (Richard again) explained. Yes, I had moved the mountain. The concern arose because after I had accepted the assignment, it was as though a fog rolled in, covering me and the mountain I was to move. Months later, the fog had rolled away, and to the amazement of all, the mountain was gone. In the meantime, however, my peers and superiors, whose own success would be greatly affected by the result, had stood there staring at the fog, wondering what Farnsworth was up to. Although a number of others had participated in completing the project, they had seen only the small piece that directly concerned them. Outside of the fog, there had been a general nervousness that nothing was happening despite the ever-nearing project deadline. Richard concluded the discussion by presenting what has become one of my most valued situation tags: "David, you are great at moving mountains, but that is not enough. You have to learn for your sake and others who will be affected to let everyone see the truckloads of dirt going by."

I realized that this criticism was well deserved. I had become so focused on getting the job done and had seen it in my mind as so well-organized and moving forward so successfully that I had not bothered to inform subordinates or to report to peers or superiors on its progress. They had been left to worry in the dark.

Complying with the **Truckloads of Dirt Requirement** remains difficult for me. I sometimes feel that stopping to report is a waste of time, and resources would be better spent actually getting something done. I admit, however, that I was recently humbled as I watched a product manager push the rushed development of a new product. Despite the rush, she required each group that managed any related dependency or contribution to attend a weekly review. It turned out to be the most effective product development in recent company history, and the well-planned reporting sessions were a significant and valid part of the process.

Besides teaching me my responsibility to report, Richard taught me how to manage what I expected from those reporting to me. I had adopted the same approach toward my subordinates I had taken myself: With people I can trust, I will let them run a project until completion. Let them move mountains; truckloads of dirt are boring. However, this approach simply left both their peers and my peers in the dark. The people on the sideline did not necessarily have my basis for confidence that a project that would affect them was moving forward. I have had to adjust to a planned reporting system not just for my sake, but for the sake of the greater good.

The **Truckloads of Dirt Requirement** has its dark side, and the tag should be used to watch for and avoid these negative manifestations as well.

I recently watched a new group vice president take on a small but significant operation at a fast-paced, growing concern. He was brilliantly prepared to advise management on critical strategic aspects of the business, but equally unprepared to manage his group as they tried to contribute on a day-to-day operational basis. Because of his insecurity as a manager, he began not only to expect to see the truckloads of dirt but also to stop them to inspect how they were loaded and test the pressure on each tire of each truck. To make matters worse, he would sometimes close the inspection station for days at a time and then suddenly demand not only to see current loads but to have trucks that had already gone by return. His micromanagement diminished the effectiveness of the whole group and eventually destroyed its morale.

Another negative arises when one places too much focus on reporting rather than doing so that reporting becomes the primary rather than a subordinate activity. I remember reading a report that certain officers in the Pentagon forbade the use of PowerPoint. Subordinates were spending more time preparing slides to report what they had done or were planning to do than in actually doing anything.

In a similar vein, I had a colleague who required that his admin call him every day if she did not see him in the office before a certain time (apparently believing that phone lines are unidirectional, he would not call her). Soon the admin spent the first hour or so of any day the boss was away from the office trying to think up something relevant to say on the call she was required to make. Since he traveled frequently, she wasted many hours. Eventually she figured out how to make the call when it was unlikely he could answer the phone and left the message "nothing to report," fulfilling the requirement but totally defeating any purpose it may have had. (See **Darley's Law** and the **360-Degree Temptation**.)

The **Truckloads of Dirt Requirement** Restatement: It is not enough to get the job done. Let subordinates, peers, and superiors have the comfort of seeing the work progress. As managers (and parents), set and hold yourself to reasonable expectations for reporting, avoiding both micromanagement and **Darley's Law** or effects from the **360-Degree Temptation**.

CHAPTER 9

The Escape Velocity Query

I am a child of the Cold War and its constant companion, the Space Race. When the Russians succeeded in placing a satellite in low earth orbit (Sputnik), we were lectured in school about the nation's need to "catch up." Those of us who were geeky enough became rocket scientists on the spot. The basic components of black powder were available off the shelf at any drugstore, and we shared recipes for other fuels: caramelized sugar and potassium nitrate melted together (careless construction causes flash fires), aluminum powder (hard to get), or just plain old sulfur, charcoal, and saltpeter (slightly moistened and cast into cardboard tubes). We soon learned the harsh reality that there is little difference between a rocket and a bomb, but as our understanding of chemistry and physics improved, we were occasionally rewarded with spectacular launches instead of thundering blasts and with significantly fewer burns that we disguised, for our mothers' sakes, as zits.

With each successful launch our ambitions grew, and soon we were dreaming of putting something (a living something if possible: grasshopper, mouse, sibling) into space. It was about this time that our math caught up with our chemistry, and we were confronted with the weighty reality of escape velocity and its corollaries. Our ardor for investing hard-earned cash in what in the end would simply be ever-more-expensive fireworks soon cooled as quickly as the ashes of our failures. Putting any object even remotely close to space was far beyond anything any of us was willing to invest in time, money, or risk, and besides, no one was willing to give us access to the really good stuff like LOX and liquid hydrogen anyway.

To put it simply, escape velocity is achieved when the negative force pulling an object toward a body (in this case the gravity of Earth) and the positive force driving it away from that body (the rocket's thrust) equal zero. At that point, the thrust can be turned off and the rocket will continue into space, freed from the restraints of its earthly origins. With lesser velocities, we can place objects in low earth orbit, going round and round the earth many times a day, or stationary orbit, much higher and circling the earth just once a day in sync with the earth's rotation so as to appear to be going nowhere.

The ultimate kicker to our space ambitions was to learn that even if we could escape the meager gravity of Earth, unless we radically increased velocity at a great expense of energy, our launch vehicle would still eventually fall, not to the hard, cold reality of Earth, but to the much warmer and totally destructive fire of the sun.

Most of my friends and I gave up on rockets; we are not astronauts and don't work for NASA. However, what I learned during my "October Sky" period became the basis of many of my favorite metaphors, including the **Escape Velocity** tag. We use a variation of this tag when we say that a project or purpose "didn't get off the ground." I use it more broadly to look for the difference between projects that succeed versus those that fail and to evaluate the way resources were or were not—or whether they should or should not continue to be—appropriated.

Lost to history for most of us is the fact that Facebook was not the first even moderately successful social networking site. In 1999 I participated in the launch of MyFamily.com, a site for "family and friends" networking that, for its time, was wildly successful. This was in those early days when using the Internet for anything, let alone social networking, was still in "early adoption." The site reached one million registered users in 164 days, unheard of at the time. Wow! So where did it go? Why didn't it take off? Many reasons. They included funding failing as the Internet bubble burst. Behavioral tracking and online advertising were in their infancy. No one was sure that social networking would ever support a legitimate business model. The company that created the site and several other social networks eventually directed its investment toward a more proven and now very successful business model that allowed it to grow into a publicly traded company. As of right now, MyFamily.com still exists but is in "low earth orbit" with the likelihood of no new investment, which means it may eventually burn on reentry.

In the early days of NASA, launch failure was more common than not. As new rocket types were tested, crash and burn was the order of the day until bugs were worked out. The possible analogies for a business, family, or social environment are many. Fuel problems—insufficient investment. Guidance system failures—bad management. Testing too early—bad product rushed to market or a relationship put under pressure too soon. Many rockets became bombs because of minor systems failures, the most tragic of which led to the loss of shuttle crews.

This tag causes me to continually ask, "What is the difference between reaching escape velocity and simply failing to launch? Why does a business or division that is set up to 'orbit' on its own quickly merge back into the welcoming glare of some wealthy corporate sun?"

This rocket-related tag also has a corollary that I find useful. An early NASA debate was between BDRs (big dumb rockets) and manned flight. In early orbital flights, the human factor was included for human interest, and even years later, much of what has been done with the shuttle could have been done much more cheaply by BDRs: computer-guided, unmanned rockets. Other things could not have been. The Hubble Space Telescope would have remained a failure without human repairmen. But it is fair, and even wise, to ask, "How much of an endeavor can be accomplished by careful preplanning and implementation, and how much and when will post-launch guidance become crucial?" Until they begin their projects after achieving orbit, a shuttle crew is simply weight, and they, their life-support systems, and their means of return cost incredible quantities of fuel. Indeed, most of the fuel burned by a rocket is used to lift the weight of the fuel that hasn't burned yet. Again, it's worth asking how much of the cost of any new, or even ongoing, endeavor goes to lifting or supporting dead weight. Do we shoot our space stations up into orbit in large chunks in a shuttle cargo bay or build more slowly with cheaper but less spectacular BDRs?

There are times and places for both. The human factor in space flight is meaningful because it *is* a human factor. While there have been many launch and recovery failures, probably hundreds, we remember three: two shuttle disasters and *Apollo* 13, the former because of the lives lost, the latter for the lives saved (we older people also remember *Apollo* 11—look it up). How much more efficient, but how much less human, would our very lives be without the "human" factor? We value putting ourselves at risk so we can claim the consequent rewards as our own. I have generally given up on rockets (though we do have a family launch of real ones each Fourth of July, compliments of Estes Industries). I have not given up on the wonders of the possibilities of a successful launch and what it is like to really, really get something "off the ground" and keep it there.

The **Escape Velocity** Query: Ask yourself when starting a new project what must be invested to ensure success. If a project falters, is it worth adding more "fuel," or should it be allowed to "burn on re-entry"? Is a project a BDR or a shuttle effort? What is the root cause of a failure to launch, and can it be corrected for the next attempt?

CHAPTER 10

In the Loop, in the Noose

At an Internet company I worked for, new products were introduced in long meetings of high-level executive staff. I sat through enough of them to become rather tech savvy and to know which product elements were likely to raise legal issues and so need my closer attention. After one meeting where many of those potential issues came to light, I grabbed the product manager and strongly suggested that I continue to be involved during early stages of product development so any legal issues could be dealt with before the product structure was set in stone. "Don't worry," he replied. "We'll give you access to..." He named some network-based planning and tracking system that the development engineers used to plot progress in a product's development. "That will keep you in the loop."

Bells, whistles, sirens. What I heard was, "By giving you access to this unfathomably complex tracking system, I feel I have met any obligation to keep you informed and all responsibility for resolving any legal issue that we may create is now yours with no further input on my part." When I got back to my desk, I immediately scheduled weekly one-on-ones with him and key members of the development group until development, testing, and product launch were concluded.

I use the **Rikki-Tikki-Tavi Imperative** as a tag to remind me when and what I need to learn to move any particular aspect of my work, play, or life forward. **In the Loop, in the Noose**, though similar, is different enough that I made it a separate tag. It relates less to what I want to learn or feel I need to learn than to what responsibilities and liabilities arise as a result of something I actually do learn or should know. By being in the loop, how much am I in the noose?

The concept of responsibility based on knowledge is one that pervades legal thinking. Even in the fake environment of TV legal dramas we hear these ominous words in the prosecutor's opening statement: "We intend to prove that the defendant knowingly . . ." or ". . . knew or should have known . . ." The prosecutor then goes on to describe some heinous crime or moral outrage. Being responsible for what we know and how we respond or don't respond based on that knowledge is bad enough, but being responsible for something we "should have known"?

How do we know what we should know if we don't know it yet? This question raises the marvelously confusing issue of status liability. A person who is a director or officer of, or counsel to a company, as a result of that status, is presumed to know certain things about that company and be in control of its behavior. Those people are in the noose because of what they should know, whether they actually know it or not. Suddenly, the **Rikki-Tikki-Tavi Imperative** kicks in hard.

This **Loop/Noose** tag became critical to me because I was once simultaneously the responsible officer for several dozen international holding companies that were subsidiaries of my main client. During that time I thought a great deal about consequences in connection with those companies. I didn't want a situation to arise that would prevent my visiting France or Italy or a lot of places that I really enjoyed because of some screw-up relating to one of those companies. Recently, U.S.-based officers of Google found themselves in exactly that situation when they were accused of crimes in Italy based on what they should have known about an abusive YouTube video. Whether fair or not, status creates liability.

Most of you may never be the responsible officer of a company, and the consequences of status liability I describe may seem unlikely. However, most of us actually do take on significant status liability: we become parents. The idea that we are responsible for the acts or inaction of another person from their birth until they are sixteen or eighteen or twenty-one, depending on the circumstances, should frighten, or at least encourage, us into becoming well informed about what that child, angel or demon, is up to.

That's enough about liability for what we should know but might not. The **Loop/Noose** tag also serves as a reminder that once I know something, like it or not, inaction or silence is not an option, no matter how much I would prefer that route. One of my most frustrating professional failures resulted from responding with silence. A client required me to work with Harry, a consultant I neither liked nor respected. Early in that relationship I received a letter from him (this was in the days of paper) outlining a plan of action he proposed. His plan was so contrary to what I believed we had agreed upon that I was furious. But rather than responding immediately, I decided to wait until I could calm down and be civil in my response. As things turned out, I should have at least responded by saying I reserved the right to respond. Unfortunately, Harry took advantage of my silence, indicating to the client that my silence must be seen as acquiescence. I was stuck with the consequences. I learned that if it's my neck in the noose as a result of being in the loop, I don't want to leave the fate of that neck in the hands of someone else.

I quoted in the **Rikki-Tikki-Tavi Imperative** essay the oft-stated aphorism "Knowledge is power." The other side of that coin is that knowledge is risk, and the risk created by any bit of knowledge is likely to be equal to the power it might convey. We can choose to not know what we should. We can also choose not to act on what we do know. What we can't choose is that there be no consequence related to our knowledge. If we are in the loop, we are likely in the noose and need to act before our necks are, at least metaphorically, stretched.

The **In the Loop, in the Noose** Restatement: You have the responsibility to know what you should know and act upon that knowledge. You have liability for both what you know and what you should know, and you cannot avoid responsibility or liability by inaction.

Tagging Tip: An Ounce of Prevention . . .Tag your experiences and knowledge at the level that will make the most difference.

Creating situation tags to help us identify recurring problems or opportunities will only be useful if we recognize the situation before negative results we could prevent occur or the opportunity is lost. As a child I lived on what was for us a farm; Dad owned an acre in the middle of a much larger cultivated area. Each summer, our job as children was to keep our flower and vegetable gardens weed free. We were reminded each spring that it was much less work to pluck up a little weed than to hoe down a well-rooted one. This was particularly true of clover. In the arid area where we lived, clover, if allowed to sprout and left for more than a few days, would send out a tap root six feet or more, seeking water deep under the otherwise parched topsoil.

We were soon convinced that pulling up young shoots was well worth the effort compared to digging out a massive tap root, particularly since even the smallest branch root, if left, would grow back into an even tougher plant. Situation tagging allows me, and will help you, identify both problems and opportunities early in their development and use early intelligent intervention to prevent root problems or having to back track to take advantage of missed opportunity.

CHAPTER 11

Nothing Sucks (But Almost Everything Leaks)

I was taken aback when my brother, a generally conservative dresser, appeared at a family gathering in a white T-shirt emblazoned with "NOTHING SUCKS!" in bold, black capitals. Curious, I got him alone for a moment and asked for enlightenment. He explained that it was a freebie from a convention for physical chemists he had recently attended (He's a physical chemist himself.). It was produced to remind the attendees, and to allow them to loudly proclaim to the world, that the motion of matter, particularly fluids, is caused by a pressure imbalance. Matter moves from a higher-pressure state to a lower-pressure state because that pressure exists, not from a lack of pressure. No pressure, no motion. Fluid motion is push, not pull. More broadly stated, vacuums, cold, and dark are not stuff; they are the absence of stuff--a lack of matter in the case of vacuums and energy in the case of light and heat. The "but almost everything leaks" corollary I added to remind myself how difficult it is, because of the presence of pressures in the form of various types of energy, to maintain a state of nothing. Since that discussion with my brother, **Nothing Sucks** has become the tag describing how I analyze group dynamics.

Harriett was the best customer relations manager I have ever known, and I have known many as an employer, a fellow employee, and a customer. As an employee in the customer relations group of a company I represented, she quickly rose to be lead trainer and then head of the escalation group that handled customer relations problems that could not be resolved by the mere mortals in the first-line group. She was this good: several times I received calls from customers who had threatened us with legal action, but after working with her, they not only took no negative action but remained loyal customers and credited her with their change of heart.

Eventually, as it should have been, Harriett was promoted and went to lead an entirely different services section of the company. She did so with the same energy and ability she had displayed in her former position. The effect on the customer services group she left, however, was immediate and remarkable. Deflated, fell flat, went cold—take your pick; they all applied. It had been her energy that had kept that group together, and in the absence of that presence, the group became ineffective. Her replacement, though a competent administrator, simply didn't have her abilities and was not able to fill the vacuum caused by her absence.

Heinrich was as much the opposite of Harriet as I could imagine. His only talent that I could discern was convincing people to like him and, as a result, to carry him. He was 'Peter Principled' up the ladder until he became manager of a significant division shortly before I joined the organization at a peer level. It didn't take long for me to conclude, in the colloquial sense, that Heinrich sucked. He was pulling on the talents, energy, and efforts of those around him to create the appearance of his own success. At one point, his boss even came to me and specifically asked if I would please expend more effort to cover for Heinrich's problems (screw-ups). Without significant effort by others, the push to ensure the success of what Heinrich should have been doing, he simply would have failed. Only the energy of those around him, myself included, allowed him to appear to succeed.

As I look at both Heinrich and Harriett with a degree of distance, I find that examining those very different situations from the **Nothing Sucks** point of view is enlightening. It is clear that the positive aspects of those Heinrich gathered around him supported his apparent success; they kept him afloat (to use a water pressure analogy) and allowed his ego to remain inflated (air pressure this time). Harriett, on the other hand, had so successfully filled the needs of her group that she may have left little room for others to grow as they might have otherwise. She filled the space which, when she left, became the vacuum.

In a more general sense, I enjoy watching a group and using the tag to identify who are the pumps and who are the vacuums. Stereotyping? Labeling? Yes. But useful in understanding a group's dynamics.

This tag has uses beyond personnel evaluations. (In fact, I've found it's a useful way of looking at almost everything—I say *almost* because I haven't looked at everything yet.)

For example, it's easy to think, and I think we often do, of motivators from the "suck" point of view: "If I offer money, they will come." But I have learned through a couple of experiences that money really isn't everything, at least not all the time. I visited a country in West Africa where inflation was so bad that I had to carry two shopping bags (the big kind with handles) full of money to pay for a taxi ride. Even at that, the driver was reluctant to take the money and suggested alternate forms of payment (cigarettes or booze), which I didn't have. The push of another motivator would have been more effective than the pull of money. On another occasion, I was in Moscow during a particularly severe shortage of everything. Being willing to pay more got you nowhere; paying more for what doesn't exist doesn't get it anymore than paying what one would if it were there in abundance. (OK, economists, I know that paying more might motivate someone to make it available, but that presumes factors not then in evidence and is another story.)

I wonder if as a society we have come to define motivation too much in the sense of suck: we describe a job "opening," a position "to be filled." We think that if we increase the reward, the pull, we will get the desired motion. "What must I offer to fill this position?" **Nothing Sucks** helps me look at wants and needs from the push side, the why of motion. "If she wants more money is it because of need or greed? Will I get better results from a carrot or a stick? What will maximize pressure?" If all we do is try to create a vacuum, we may have little control over what moves in to fill it. If we examine the pressures around us, we can customize releases for them and so control what moves and in what direction.

This leads us, briefly, to the corollary: **Everything leaks**. We have all experienced getting the bike out now that it's summer and finding the tires flat, buying the balloons for a party a day too early and having them sink rather than float, or coming home to a cold house because the furnace failed. Systems, human ones included, lose energy. Using **Nothing Sucks** thinking to determine where the leak might be and decide the most effective point to add energy is part of the process as I use this tag.

The **Nothing Sucks** Restatement: Matter and energy move from a high-pressure to a low-pressure state. Thinking of human interactions in this way leads to an understanding of group dynamics based on push rather than pull motivation.

CHAPTER 12

The Chaos Disclaimer

Now that you've read a few of the essays and have a feel for how tags work, I want to discuss the tag for all tags, one that applies to, and in a sense qualifies, all the others.

One of the few books I have read more than once is *Chaos*, by James Gleick. I read the book several times because the topic is fascinating but also, I admit, because it is difficult to grasp. We have all experienced what we call chaos—disastrous disorder, confounding confusion, unmitigated mess. This, however, is not the chaos Mr. Gleick describes. His book is about the math, science, and real-world effects of patterned disorder or disorderly patterns: patterns that exist but don't repeat and that are often easily formulated but may be impossible to predict. I have adopted three "rules" of chaos as situation tags, though they might be called "special situation" tags because they also apply to situation tagging in general. They are also interrelated, which is why I am describing them together. With apologies to Mr. Gleick if I am mistaken in my understanding of these "rules," but wanting to give credit for the insight he has provided, here we go.

The name of the first might sound a little intimidating: **Sensitive Dependence on Initial Conditions**. This rule is often alluded to with the statement "butterfly wings in Beijing." The premise is that a butterfly flying in Beijing will move a number of air molecules one way or another, which in turn affects the flow of other molecules, and on and on until that butterfly has influenced weather in the North Pacific several weeks later. "Sensitive dependence" means that small changes in input may have massive effects on output. "Initial conditions" is the status of something at the time of that input, and a critical factor is that these initial conditions can exist only once and will never, ever exist again.

I had an extensive internal debate about initial conditions while I was a student living in Vienna, Austria. Shortly after I moved into a small apartment on Stumpergasse I learned that if I had lived there sixty years earlier, Adolf Hitler would have been my neighbor. Being on the street where he lived led me to learn why he was there and the results of his activities at the time. He had come to Vienna at about the same age I was when I lived there with the hope of studying at the Academy of Art. He was not admitted based on the cityscapes he presented as samples of his work and was told that he should apply to study architecture. However, he couldn't study architecture because he had dropped out of high school. He eventually became a homeless wanderer in Vienna until joining the German army in WWI. I could not help but wonder each day as I passed his apartment building how the world would have been different if Hitler had been accepted to either course of study. Likely, he would never have gone to Munich, never become . . . Sensitive dependence simply means that if any "what if" had been different, the results would compound in a cascading and unpredictable way.

This disclaimer may appear to negate the whole premise and promise of this book; i.e., that situations reoccur and that we can learn to manage them based on prior learning. Actually, it should simply refine and focus our thinking as we move from the general (the tag) to the specific (the actual situation at hand). The rule to remember when creating and applying situation tags is this: Yes, this has all happened before, and it will all happen again, but this time it won't happen *exactly* as it did before. While we're busy applying all the knowledge and wisdom that a tag brings to mind, at the same time, we need to be sensitive to differences. A situation that looks so familiar it calls up a tag (initial conditions) may develop in an entirely and unpredictably different way (sensitive dependence). But don't be discouraged. Human beings love to ignore chaos theory and are very likely to act and react in fairly predictable ways. Beyond that, you can create (and this book exists to encourage you to) continuous intelligent interference. We reset initial conditions again and again, redirecting the dependent result. The **Sensitive Dependence** tag is a caution flag, not a stop sign.

The second element of my Chaos Disclaimer is the **Strange Attractors** tag. The strange attractor model predicts the path of a line that, if viewed in two dimensions, appears to curve back and forth and cross itself many times. However, in three-dimensional space, this line will never intersect itself, no matter how close it seems to come to doing so. The application to tagging is actually fairly straightforward. It's simply this: because we differ in so many aspects of our lives, no two of us really see a situation in exactly the same way. If two people read this book and each has an "ah-ha" moment, recognizes one of the situations in their personal experience, and later describes to the other a situation using the tag, they will come close to a mutual understanding. However, that understanding intersects, metaphorically, only in the broader, two-dimensional sense.

I worked closely with a group engaged in a massive translation project, and while not a translator myself, I was frequently asked whether this or that word in the target language represented more closely the original English meaning. I learned that language is a "strange attractor" element and that with so many choices of words to express an idea in another language, understanding of the translated work would come close to, but not fully intersect, all the nuances contained in the original. But again, humans are not doomed by chaos theory to never work together. Although we may never actually "intersect," we get close enough to successfully interact, and that is usually sufficient.

This brings us to the third chaos tag: **Fractalization**. This is the concept that a pattern can and will repeat on macro to micro scales. A mountain is like a boulder is like a rock is like a pebble is like a grain of sand. I have a photo of a flower—beautifully formed with leaves, petals, and everything else that makes a flower—growing in a gravel bed. It appears ready to plucked and be placed in an arrangement. However, a second picture, where my fingers appear on either side of the flower, reveals that the entire plant is not as tall as half the thickness of my finger, and the gravel is very fine sand.

An illustration I like because it awakens an understanding of point of view is to ask and answer, "How long is the coast of California?" To a sailor it is the distance from the Mexican border to the Oregon border. To an oceanographer who is interested in going into the major bays to see what is there, the distance becomes longer as the borders of the bays and inlets are included. To a cartographer who must accurately map each bay and inlet within each bay and inlet, the coast is longer still. To an ecologist who is worried about the effects of runoff for all sources flowing into the Pacific from California, the coast includes the banks of every river and every tributary to every river and every rivulet that flows into each tributary and eventually the course of every raindrop that falls on the west side of the Sierra Divide.

The application? Each person will take measure of each situation from a more or less macro-to-micro point of view, but no two people will see a situation exactly the same way. But again, no reason for despair. Despite our differences, we humans seek universals, and most of us will never try to measure the edges of every river or predict the course of a raindrop. Be forewarned, not discouraged.

The **Chaos Disclaimer** Restatement: In recognizing that a situation fits into a tag, also recognize that (1) No two situations are truly identical and that those that start out similar may end very disparate; (2) No two people working to resolve a situation will see it exactly the same way because (3) Each observer will have a macro or micro point of view that depends upon their own interests and experience.

CHAPTER 13

The Axe in the Ceiling Silliness

A fairytale I remember from my childhood is the basis for this tag. It is the story of a family whose beautiful daughter has become engaged. It is a "Once upon a time in the olden days" story, so the mother, rather than going to the refrigerator to get refreshments for the engagement party, goes down into the dark, cool cellar. Raising her candle to light her way, she sees, with great dread, an axe stuck in one of the ceiling beams. Immediately she begins a "parade of horribles" in her mind. "What if that axe falls out and hits me? What if when my daughter comes to fetch something from the cellar, that axe falls and kills her? I will never have any grandchildren. What if I have a grandchild and he comes down here, and the axe falls and kills him? The death of a dear grandchild would be more than I could bear." Soon she is sitting on the floor, weeping and wailing at the loss of her great-grandchildren who will never be because of this axe in the ceiling.

Eventually, her husband notices her absence, comes to find her, and is forced to hear her parade of horribles. He chimes in with a few horribles of his own and joins in with gnashing of teeth. The daughter notices that her parents are missing, goes in search of them, and is soon alongside them, mourning their death, her death, and the tragedy of future generations who will never be. In some versions of this story, the whole engagement party ends up in the cellar, flooding the floor with their tears. In due course, the bridegroom misses the bride, family, and the rest of the guests and ventures down to the cellar. Amazed at the grief that has befallen his engagement party, he seeks out his bride-to-be and demands to know the cause of all this distress. She, joined by others in the party, raises a trembling finger to point to the axe and recites the long parade of horribles. "Oh," says the bridegroom and reaches up and pulls the axe from the ceiling.

In some versions of the story, the groom walks away in disgust. In others, he marries into this family of Sillies, further justifying the use of that very appropriate word in this tag.

One of my own favorite experiences with this "much ado about little" occurred when, wondering what it would be like to earn my living as something other than as a lawyer, I became program manager for the large-account sales program of a software publisher. When the program was developed, it was decided that because the large customers served were so important, an account manager would be involved with each account from beginning to end. With each new sale, the sales rep introduced the account manager, who then managed every aspect of the account. These account managers were skilled at relationship management and were soon in cozy with the relevant procurement specialists at the companies they were assigned to. Not too far into the program's implementation, and about the time I joined the group, it became apparent that there was a flaw somewhere in the process.

Sales were climbing at a record pace, customers were expressing great satisfaction with the program, and relationships seemed solid and improving. However, receivables were out of control. Our product was selling like hotcakes, but we weren't being paid. It was soon apparent that while the account managers were doing a great job at schmoozing their procurement counterparts, they weren't good at demanding money. Demanding money was seen as relationship negative, and besides, pushing the procurement guys for payment wasn't productive; they ordered the product, but they didn't control payment. Procurement people saw no advantages in pushing their own payables people; that was a different department. Collections became the axe in the ceiling.

As the scope of the problem (a ton of cash) became increasingly clear, meetings to discuss solutions followed meetings to discuss manpower demands by the account management group (with more people, they would schmooze their procurement counterparts even more). Someone proposed training programs to teach account managers how to demand payment. Put a payment specialist on the account management team; send training materials to procurement counterparts; create an automated reminder process to be administered by another headcount. The common denominator seemed to be more: more people, more cost, more complexity. Finally, after more wasted management cycles than I care to remember, someone pulled the axe out of the ceiling. Accounts receivable belonged in finance, not in sales. Finance could demand payment directly from the customer's accounts payable department, with no direct contact with the procurement group unless there was substantial default. Duh.

Frankly, that was what the customers had expected. Account managers and procurement specialists could schmooze away about next-quarter purchases to their hearts' content, and no new headcount was required because finance had a fully automated system. The only issue that remained was "Who was the idiot who put that blankety-blank axe in the ceiling in the first place?" Territorial squabbles and empire building, that's who; but that's another story.

Another of my favorite axe stories comes from my brother-in-law Bill. In his first job out of business school, he spent much of his time doing statistical analysis for the tax manager at a Fortune 500 company. One day he asked his boss, John, how he had come to be there. John replied that some years before, the IRS had begun a series of deep-dive audits of the company. Accounting practices were challenged, resources were diverted to reviewing years of past returns and books, and just as one issue was resolved, the IRS case manager managed to find another. The company began to feel it was being persecuted. Meetings multiplied. "Should we totally revise our accounting practices? Should we set up a special project audit team? Should we complain to our congressman that we're being made a special case without justification?"

"Moaning and groaning all around," John said.

"So," Bill speculated, "they brought you in as a specialist even the IRS would respect and stay away from?"

"Sort of," John replied. "They did solve their problem by making me an offer I couldn't refuse: three times what I was making as their IRS auditor!" The company had been John's hobbyhorse, and as soon as they hired him away, no one at the IRS wanted to touch them because John anticipated and could readily respond to every possible IRS attack.

A simple, homier example: My friend Hank moved to Southern California and bought a house with a beautiful, mature yard for his kids to play in. Soon after they moved in, his wife recognized that a marvelous flowering shrub that she so admired was oleander, beautiful indeed, but deadly poisonous. She had read that people fairly frequently got sick and occasionally died from using oleander twigs to roast wieners or marshmallows or to make willow whistles. She wondered how to train the kids to avoid the oleander and then mused about what might happen if friends or family visited for a backyard barbeque and whether she would remember to warn them. Hank's wife continued to worry out loud every time she saw the shrub. After they had lived in the house for a couple of weeks, she looked out at the yard one Saturday morning and found the oleander gone—dug up, carted away, and replaced by a harmless rhododendron. She never said a word.

Often when moaning and groaning starts, if we stop to look carefully, we can identify a single core dislocation, some relatively minor thing that is out of place, which, if moved or rectified, will prevent the parade of horribles from ever beginning. The **Axe in the Ceiling** tag can reminds us of the first **Chaos Disclaimer**: small changes in initial conditions can cause radical corrections to prevent what might but shouldn't be or create what should. The trick is recognizing the axe and how easy it is to remove it.

Of course, as with many tags, the **Axe in the Ceiling** tag contains a preventative warning. Even as a child, I remember wondering when I heard this story, "How in the world did that axe get into the ceiling?" (As my vocabulary changed with age, the question changed, I am ashamed to admit, to "What stupid idiot did that?"). In the first example I cited in this section, it became clear that the manager of the sales representative support group had placed an axe in her group's ceiling by trying to take on a responsibility that was outside the scope of their competence as she attempted to expand her own apparent responsibility. As a parent, I would never plant an oleander in my yard. Avoiding IRS audits? Well, that is another story.

The **Axe in the Ceiling Silliness** Query: Is there a core problem or dependency that, if resolved or changed, would essentially disarm the situation?

Tagging tip: Cutting to the Core: Learn to tag causes, not just or even primarily consequences.

Situation tags will be most useful when they identity a core issue, not just a consequence. The most difficult problem with serious problem solving is misidentifying the problem. I worked for some years for a large, fast-growing multinational. During one period of particularly rapid growth, the board changed CEOs. The new CEO spent his first few months doing a deep dive into every aspect of the company, and we all worked extra hard to demonstrate our dedication to the business and its success. He then rather abruptly called a meeting of the senior staff. He opened by saying, "Wow, I have never seen so many people working so hard . . ." The smiles that had formed on our faces disappeared as he finished the sentence: ". . . at doing the wrong things." In fact, in my division, the director had been defining our job success through effort, not accomplishment, and this apparently was true throughout the company. Our new CEO instructed the management group to stop and analyze exactly what their group should be trying to accomplish.

In the debate between work hard vs. work smart, situation tags are absolutely about working smart. When a tag pops into your mind, it should come with a clear message: I have seen this issue before; I understand the problem or opportunity it defines; I have solved this problem or taken advantage of this opportunity or seen it done, and as a result, I can do what needs to be done faster, better, and more effectively.

The alternative is facing not only the same situations but often the same poor results again and again. Situation tags are more about taking control of outcomes than waiting to deal with effects. Avoiding negative consequences is best accomplished not by ducking or correcting the consequences after a chain of events has already run its course, but by stopping a chain of events from ever occurring. Situation tags are most useful when you look beyond avoiding negative consequences and begin to manage causes. One of the earliest lessons a child learns is "Mom's mad" and its corollary, "Avoid Mom." Maturity begins when we learn not just to avoid Mom when she is mad, but to avoid making Mom mad. As I have adopted situation tags, I have tried to look toward causality and learning to correct or direct at that level, not just at the consequence level.

Certainly, managing consequences is often necessary and sometimes imperative (as you'll see in the **Rattlesnake Wrongheadedness**). However, true change occurs only as we recognize and manage causation. As you create your own set of situation tags, look to recognize and resolve causes, not just consequences. The real bottom line to the **Mad Mom** tag is "How can I avoid making Mom mad?" and not just "How can I avoid mad Mom?"

CHAPTER 14

The Berezina Revision

As fall fell in 1812, Napoleon, who was occupying an abandoned Moscow, was wise enough to realize that, although the Russians were not attacking, he was about to be defeated by those great protectors of Russia's heartland: cold and distance. The Russians had adopted a scorched-earth policy, and with winter about to block his supply lines, Napoleon's French army would be left thousands of miles from the nearest support with nothing to eat, wear, or shoot. Napoleon withdrew, with the Russian army now dogging his heals and giving battle wherever circumstances or geography slowed his retreat.

After two long months of being hounded but not engaged, in late November, Napoleon found himself in what is now central Belarus, up against the Berezina River. A large Russian force had arrived before him, crossed the river, taken up positions on the heights above it, and destroyed the only bridge. The nearest ford was twenty miles away. A second Russian army was closing on Napoleon's rear. Much to the disadvantage of the French, normally bitter and extremely cold temperatures had moderated, and the ice on the river had softened to the point that it broke under the weight of an average man, let alone the ponderous burden of horses, supply wagons, and cannons.

Under constant bombardment and musket fire, the French succeeded in bridging the river, and Swiss mercenaries opened a bridgehead on the Russian-controlled side. As you can imagine, pushing an entire army across a single bridge carried serious consequences. The Russians were able to focus fire on a narrow column and attack the French at the rear where those not yet across crowded together in indefensible positions. Many of the French were forced into, or out of desperation took to, the ice-choked waters, and thousands drowned. While the French eventually broke out, the battle had cost as many as 25,000 casualties among the French combatants and more than an equal number of losses among the French support personnel and civilian camp followers. Of the Swiss mercenaries, who had numbered 1,800 at the beginning of the battle and who had been the first to force their way across the river and later also constituted the rear guard, fewer than 300 survived. Berezina was catastrophic to Napoleon and particularly to those Swiss mercenaries, whose exploits are well recorded because one of Napoleon's Swiss adjutants wrote what is likely the most accurate history of the retreat in general and of that battle specifically. For the record, most historians wonder that any of the French escaped that battle alive or un-captured, and there is little praise given the Russian leadership for letting Napoleon escape.

Some 178 years later, I found myself standing in deep snow in the center of that battlefield on the banks of the Berezina. I had been in Minsk on business with Franz, a colleague and friend who, among his many other talents and attributes was a high-ranking officer in the Swiss military and an avid military historian. To my surprise, Franz, who in general focused only on work, insisted that we take a day off and travel from Minsk to the Berezina. On the drive out, he explained that he had carefully studied the battle I referred to. He greatly admired the Swiss leadership at the Berezina and the courage of those few Swiss who played such a large role in saving part of the French army.

So on that bright but bitterly cold afternoon, I traipsed back and forth with Franz as he pointed out where the bridge must have been, the heights the Russians had controlled, and the place where his valiant Swiss predecessors had created the bridgehead on this side and held the Russians at bay on that side. His knowledge of the battle was encyclopedic, his grasp of the geography complete, and his enthusiasm for the military meaning of each element of the battle (It raged for several days.) contagious and compelling.

After we had been on the battlefield for close to an hour and I had been instructed on the who, what, where, why, and how in glowing military detail, we were distracted by the sight of a man approaching on one of the strangest conveyances I had ever seen. It was a horse-drawn sledge, low to the ground and simply made of rough wooden planks with wide, solid runners. The man who drove it was lying on his stomach on a pile of straw, guiding the horse with long double reins. As I watched, I was convinced that I could have seen the same scene if I had been there five hundred or even a thousand years before. The sledge drew up beside us and stopped. The driver stood and began to speak to us in rapid Russian. Fortunately, our driver/translator, who had watched us relive the battle from the sidelines, had seen our visitor and caught up with us at about the same time. He explained that the man was a local farmer who had come to inquire what we were doing wandering around in the middle of his pasture. Franz explained that he was interested in military history and had come to see the battlefield.

"Did you know this was a famous battlefield?" he inquired.

Know? He more than knew. The man's family had lived in the area for hundreds of years, and the stories of that battle involving his ancestors and those of others in the nearby village had become legend. We learned how the Russians, as part of their scorched-earth strategy, had burned what would have been life-sustaining crops, followed by the burning of the forests, sheds, barns, and houses by Russians and French as they sought firewood against the bitter cold of that November. Stories of courage were replaced by stories of carnage, honor was supplanted by horror. To this man and his neighbors, the Battle of Berezina is remembered as the time when great-great-grandparents almost froze or starved, followed by succeeding generations working for a century to repair the damage done by the trampling feet of hundreds of thousands of men and horses. Not only crops, barns, and houses had to be replaced, but minds that had experienced the cries of men, women, and children drowning in the river where they had been driven needed mending as well.

As we returned to the car to drive back to Minsk, my friend, a good and compassionate man, was visibly shaken. What had been an abstract study of strategy and the valiant efforts of his Swiss compatriots had been supplemented with an understanding of the effects of war on flesh-and-blood individuals, images still vivid despite the participants being long dead. Franz was no longer the proud Swiss colonel; he became the silent, contemplative observer of the worst that humanity has to offer. He had undergone the **Berezina Revision.**

Revision is a word we generally use to describe making changes, but this tag takes the word to its root level, meaning "to see again." Often, as in the case I described, our ability to really re-view requires us to see through the eyes of another. One of my most significant "revisions" happened during a visit to Moscow during the early 1990s. As I had studied late-European history, Joseph Stalin emerged as one of the true monsters of modern times, or any time, for that matter. His persecution of his own people in the gulags has been detailed by Solzhenitsyn and others. Less well known is his genocide of the Kulaks, which resulted in more than ten million deaths, mostly from starvation.

During that Moscow visit, the flood of Western visitors following perestroika had overcrowded all the hotels in the city and surrounding area. As I phoned Olga, my translator, to tell her I would have to cancel my trip, she proposed a solution by inviting me to stay with her family. Desperate to get on with my work, I agreed and upon arrival was welcomed to a modest flat in what had once been one of the better districts of Moscow. Olga, (a bright young student of nineteen), her parents, and her grandmother lived there in three rooms and a small kitchen. One bedroom became mine for the night.

At breakfast the next morning I met the grandmother for the first time, a frankly dowdy, gray woman. (I had been told once that there were many beautiful Russian girls but no beautiful Russian women; life there destroyed beauty quickly.) This woman looked at me with daggers and distain. Olga noticed my discomfort and explained. Grandmother still distrusted all Westerners, particularly capitalist, American Westerners. She had never imagined meeting one, let alone sitting at breakfast with one in her own apartment. It turned out that the grandmother was the owner of the apartment; she had earned it by building, along with other young, optimistic Communists, the building in which it stood.

To those builders, Stalin was their hero for saving them from the German monsters and bringing a degree of economic stability to their war-torn world. I was sitting across from a woman who had personally known Joseph Stalin and to whom he was still that hero, despite the "de-Stalinization" that had recently occurred in the Soviet Union. While her point of view didn't change my own that Stalin was a monster, I had to recognize that her position was as real to her as mine was to me and that in dealing with and doing business in "her" culture, I needed to take that into consideration.

In the course of the thirty-five-plus years of my career, I have worked in more than seventy countries and have had to constantly keep in mind that no matter how convinced I am of my own understanding, politics, culture, faith, and everything else that makes me me and matters to me, my position is a minority point of view. I also have to remind myself that to all others I am the foreigner, and that includes not only my contacts in Beijing or Budapest, but to some degree my neighbor next door as well.

The **Berezina Revision** Restatement: In every situation involving others, there will be differences of opinion. Listen to and respect other opinions even when you are unable to agree. Always be open to revision.

CHAPTER 15

The Musket/Rifle Conflict

The evolution of arms for the common soldier has again and again changed the nature of battle. Those with superior weaponry gained an advantage until their opponents caught up. Perhaps the most disruptive change in infantry warfare was the development of the individually carried, shoulder-fired musket, a muzzle-loaded weapon shooting a lead ball pushed by an explosion of black powder.

The musket was a potent weapon not, initially, because it was efficient but because it was effective. I have seen a well-trained bowman accurately shoot more than seventeen arrows a minute. A well-trained musketeer (They were really called that.) can get off four shots per minute. The advantage of the musket over the bow and arrow was that the musket ball penetrated shields and armor, though that advantage came with limitations. A musket, besides its comparatively slow rate of fire, is also woefully inaccurate. Being able to hit a man-sized target at more than fifty yards becomes unlikely. In fact, much beyond that distance, the safest place to be would be directly in front of the barrel.

The musket was developed with a smooth bore, a steel cylinder loaded by pouring powder down the barrel and then pushing a lead ball surrounded by a cloth or paper patch down the barrel and pounding it firmly against the powder. In order to be sure that the patch and ball can enter the barrel easily, the barrel has to be larger than the ball plus patch. As it is fired, the ball literally bounces around in the barrel, and the last bounce determines the ultimate direction the ball will spin as it leaves the barrel. That spin will affect the flight of the ball.

Someone cleverly learned that if the direction of the spin of the projectile (the ball) could be controlled, the direction of flight could be determined. Enter the rifle. By cutting ridges and valleys (called lands and grooves) that twisted along the length of the barrel, the ball is made to spin, with the axis of the spin being an imaginary line down the center of the barrel. The gyroscopic effect of this spin keeps the bullet on that path, making directly in front of the rifled barrel the most dangerous place to be. By the time of the American Revolution, a good rifleman could hit a man-sized target at up to four hundred yards.

So, arm your infantry with rifles, right? Not so fast. I have already noted that a well-trained musketeer could fire four, and possibly five, shots a minute. An equally adept rifleman could likely load and fire about half that fast. The problem with a rifle is that the barrel has two diameters: the diameter of the grooves, which determines the size of the ball, and the diameter of the lands, which is smaller so as to force the ball along the lands, imparting spin. Since the "lands" diameter of the barrel is smaller than the ball, the ball must be pushed into the barrel with considerable force, "set onto the lands." This requires additional time to ram as opposed to push the ball down the barrel, resulting in a longer loading time.

The rifle had an additional problem. The grooves tended to fill up with unburned black powder residue, making it more difficult to load the rifle with each shot. With the smooth bore of the musket, much of the powder residue is removed as each new load is pushed down the barrel.

Thus, as nations decided how to arm their troops, a conflict arose: speed or accuracy? So long as the order of battle was still closely packed columns, the musket won. The point-and–shoot, "linier shotgun" approach was effective against closely packed troops at relatively short ranges. No one was in a hurry to be the first to try to take advantage of a longer first shot but with the risk that the other side could get off several more volleys while the riflemen reloaded.

The rifle developed both as a hunting tool (much better to be able to hit a deer at one hundred yards than to hope one could get lucky with a musket at a much closer range) and as a guerilla weapon—small squads of soldiers apart from the main columns taking potshots and then withdrawing to reload. Napoleon lost one of his field marshals to a remarkable shot by a British rifleman at the then-exceptional distance of five hundred yards. The marshal had been certain he was out of range.

It was several hundred years before the rifle evolved to overcome the speed-of-loading issue that allowed it to replace the musket. The first step in that evolution came with the invention of the Minié ball (though it was not "mini" in the sense of being little, nor was it a ball). Minié was a French officer who invented a bullet-shaped projectile that included a part that expanded when fired; thus it could be small enough to easily fit down a rifled barrel but expand into the grooves as the rifle was fired. Shortly thereafter, breech-loading rifles (loaded from the back of the barrel) were perfected. The ball or projectile didn't have to be forced down the barrel at all. The musket became history.

The **Musket/Rifle Conflict** tag points out several realities. One is using the right tool. On a short-range, crowded battlefield where point and shoot is adequate, use a musket. If hunting where accuracy at range is necessary, use a rifle. I use the tag, however, in a more limited sense: to focus on the disparity that sometimes exists between speed and accuracy.

In a recent position I worked closely with Raymond, who thought himself in one respect the paragon of efficiency. He would respond to emails incredibly quickly. Armed with his Blackberry, he could do so from almost anywhere at almost any time. He lived in a different time zone, and I was often amazed when I would get a response to an email from him at times when I thought he would be asleep. He gained the reputation of the fastest gun in the West, until our group was joined by another Blackberry-wielding desperado who would occasionally respond even faster.

After some time dealing with Raymond, I began to question whether he had given sufficient thought to a matter before responding, and in many cases I felt that he hadn't. Certainly, when replying via Blackberry while on the move it was clear that any reference to files or cross-checking before responding had been impossible. I began to send him emails only at the end of my day with the hope that he would be asleep and therefore would not respond until the next day, hopefully after some thought on the matter in question. With the other colleague, who was in my time zone, I simply quit expecting a well-reasoned response. I learned to expect to exchange several volleys of emails before pinning down the ultimate answer, a waste of time for me and for him, from my perspective.

I have noted a similar load, point, and shoot problem in the document-drafting portion of deal negotiations. Email and computers allow us to open a document, redline it on an initial read through, and shoot it back without having to take much thought. Back in the "old days" when I began my legal practice, documents were exchanged by mail, and drafts were turned once a week rather than in a matter of minutes. We gave serious consideration to every point in a document before sending it off, not knowing when we might see it again.

Technophobe, Luddite, old fogy, you might be saying. No. I have done very well by technology. I use this tag to remind me that speed may be the enemy of accuracy and efficiency. I also use it because I have learned that people generally tend to be either musketeers or riflemen in their work styles, and noting that helps me deal with them appropriately.

I do fear that modern technology and culture are training more musketeers than riflemen. Social media and even email are pressing upon us with such demands for an immediate response that our tendency is to "point and shoot," blast a quick tweet to who knows who, or Facebook that advancing column of "friends." Our responses have to be increasingly volley-like because we really don't know whom we are trying to hit.

This tag also helps me to remember that organizations, as was the case with the most effective armies until the advent of the breach-loading rifle, need both musketeers *and* riflemen. Many of the problems we confront can be resolved by point-and-shoot methods, and speed is more efficient than accuracy. Other issues require deliberate, well-aimed solutions. The trick is to put the right weapon to work on the right front.

You have likely concluded, correctly, that I am a rifleman (see the **Second Opinion Requirement**). I admit that and recognize that it has its problems. In a 360 evaluation one of my colleagues wrote, "In meetings, Farnsworth speaks seldom and generally last, and he is always right. The fact that he always waits until he can be right means that he contributes too little to the discussion." I never felt that I was always right, but I do understand his criticism. Riflemen may wait so long for their shot that the target disappears and the shot is wasted. On the other hand, musketeers may waste their shot by simply blasting away and hitting nothing or the wrong target altogether.

The **Rifle/Musket Conflict** Query: Is the situation one in which speed or accuracy is more important? Is this person (or organization) a rifleman or a musketeer, and how can you best utilize that talent?

CHAPTER 16

The Cicarelli Choice

Ms. Cicarelli (a stage name) is a Brazilian model and TV personality. She is known to me, however, not as either of those, but as the subject of an important legal battle. It seems that Ms. C and her boyfriend, while vacationing in Spain, engaged in rather public sex. Some enterprising person sharing the beach with them filmed the whole process, and the video ended up on TV. TV distribution was short lived and the matter could have ended there, but another enterprising person posted the whole show on YouTube. (Don't bother to look up the video, there is really nothing to be seen.) It is difficult to say what might have become of that video, buried as it was among the millions or billions on that media channel, except that the boyfriend chose to bring legal action against YouTube in Brazil to force removal of the piece. The video immediately became not one among billions but "the one," as the litigation brought it global attention. The possibility that it would be repressed made that video the choice of many re-publishers. Frankly, had the video not become the center of a significant legal battle, I would never have heard about it, let alone seen it. I think that is likely the case for many eventual viewers. The choice by Ms. C and her partner to "make a big deal out of it" did, indeed, make a big deal out of it, and what might have remained relatively private became massively public. I admit wondering in this case whether increased publicity wasn't, in fact, the objective. If it wasn't, then the choice was certainly the wrong one.

Dealing with a situation where one's "rights" may have been affected but where taking action could result in unintended and possibly negative consequences raises difficult choices. On the one hand, you want justice and the protection of the law or other rules. On the other, "justice" can often be sought only in a public forum.

Another YouTube-related case comes to mind. A mother posted an unquestionably cute video of her toddler rocking out to a, for me at least, difficult to distinguish rock song that came across almost as background noise. However, the distributor representing the band that recorded the song the toddler was dancing to took offence and brought legal action against the mother for public replay of a copyrighted performance. The publicity backlash was immediate and aggressive. Where did a big bad music company get off persecuting a mother for making a video of her cute little kid and sharing it with her friends on the Internet (millions of "friends" that she doesn't know at all, but that's the nature of social networking)? This was, after all, not file sharing; no one would take that low-quality background recording and drop it onto their mp3 player in place of a purchased download. The music industry took a significant PR hit and eventually backed off.

So, is pursuing a legal or other right worth the potential public consequences? This is the quandary raised by the **Cicarelli's Choice** tag. It is not uncommon to fall back on the "Any publicity is good publicity" response. However, with the breadth, intensity, and googlized permanence of publicity that can race around the world via the Internet in an instant, the "any" response may not be responsible. In the case of Ms. C., the initial legal decision was that YouTube must pull the video. However, that decision was reversed on appeal, and the ultimate ruling was that that which is done in public may remain public. The couple's legal efforts merely assured that it would be *more* public.

As to the music industry, their reaction to the kid rocker video was difficult for me to understand. I am old enough to remember (but just barely) the payola scandals that ruined the careers of some of the country's most prominent DJs. The short story behind those scandals is that record producers were paying DJs to assure that their recordings received maximum airtime. Airtime on the radio moved the recording up the charts, radically increasing sales. Public exposure of a song was, it seems, worth paying for. In the YouTube case, however, public exposure was worth suing against. I haven't figured that one out.

As an attorney, I am regularly approached by clients who begin the conversation with, "So and so has done such and such; can we sue him?" With all the patience I can muster, I point out that litigation has significant drawbacks. It is expensive, time consuming, an emotional distraction, and most relevant to the point at hand, will inevitably result in publicity. Frequently, the response to the publicity warning will be, "But that's okay; I am right. I want to show that I am right.

Publicity will be a good thing." For those who don't find the **Cicarelli Choice** example relevant, I respond by relating the publicity consequences of the one truly famous litigation I was involved in. It's a useful example because it underscores several of the publicity risks surrounding cases about "rights."

First, it was between two prominent organizations, both of which had significant support in the community. As the publicity around the matter increased, the factions became increasingly vocal and aggressive in expressing their points of view. The two major newspapers in the city where the litigation was based took sides. For a time the publicity raised by the matter was seriously divisive to the community. I have learned to ask my clients to carefully consider whether being "right" is worth the potential negative effects proving it will have on their brand and standing in the community. In the kid rocker case, the music company may have had some arguable legal right, but in the eyes of a very global community they looked very wrong.

The second lesson I learned from my "famous" case that I try to pass on to my clients is that even if they believe that they are right and the facts are clear, someone, and possibly everyone, will get it wrong. That case resulted in my first serious interaction with the media (print and broadcast—the Internet wasn't around yet). Despite numerous press releases, briefings and clarifying phone calls, and the presence of numerous reporters at the hearings and trial, the reporting was always to some degree (and often to a great degree) factually and legally incorrect. Thus the warning: as one makes the **Cicarelli Choice** and decides whether to accept the consequences of pursuing public redress of a problem, it is wise to go review the **Chaos Disclaimer**: the matter will never, never, never work out as one expects because of lack of understanding of, let alone of control over, all of the initial conditions.

The **Cicarelli Choice** Query: Are efforts to prove a right or point of view worth the cost of both the foreseeable and unintended public side effects?

CHAPTER 17

The Rhett Retort

If you hang around our house very long, you'll hear a number of classic movie lines being quoted with relative frequency. "They're heeerrrre" usually refers to grandkids showing up. "I'll be back" is me leaving on a rock hounding trip, which worries my wife because I'll be in the deep desert by myself for longer than she thinks is safe. The line you'll hear most often, however, is the Rhett Retort: "Frankly my dear, I don't give a damn." Poor Scarlett, on the receiving end of such monumental indifference as she pleads out of fear for her future, "But Rhett, what will become of me?" We usually don't quote the question, though it reveals Scarlett's real problem: she is so full of herself, so focused on "me," that she has left no room for anyone else in her life. That, however, is another story.

To not give a damn about another human being is harsh, and my wife and I use the Rhett Retort in a broader context. It helps us remember to consider our "circle of distraction." I have to give credit here to Mr. Covey and his *Seven Habits of Highly Successful People.* He discusses the concepts of a circle of influence and a circle of concern in some detail as he reasons that it makes no sense to worry about things we have no influence over; it's a waste of time and emotional energy. I have created a typically much larger circle: the circle of distraction. *Concern* implies some real thought, perhaps even serious worry. *Distractions* are less deep and more likely simply a waste of time.

A few years ago I was involved with a group of prominent business and church leaders who were organizing a charitable relief effort in the wake of a major earthquake. In order to get us to where we needed to be quickly, one of the group made his well-appointed private jet available. As we enjoyed the comfort and dispatch with which we could board and take off compared to what we would have faced on a commercial flight, one of my companions commented on various aspects of the craft and its flight capabilities. Since he was a doctor, I was surprised at his knowledge and interest. As we discussed flying and his excitement about the subject became increasingly clear, I asked whether he was a pilot. Learning to fly seemed a logical result of his interest. With a somewhat wistful look, he said that he wasn't. He explained that it had been a great temptation, and he certainly could afford it financially. However, he had realized that had he become more involved in flying, it would have consumed him. He was afraid that flying would distract him from matters that he had determined were more important. My already deep admiration for him increased and forced me to review my own sense of what was important as opposed to what might be simply a distraction.

Distractions abound and our access to them seems to be on a rapid and steep rise. In today's world, the potential size of one's circle of distraction is immense. A hundred years ago, people had little contact with much outside of their community. For most people, life was focused on making a living, getting by. Newspapers, if you could read and afford to buy one, were the typical access to a larger world. Occasionally, the circus came to town, and for a few hours, folks were amazed and distracted by the exotic animals and performances.

Over what is a very short period in human history, we were blessed or cursed with radio, TV, computers, CDs, DVDs, the Internet, social media, and digital books. I raise the example of the circus because we now have access to a global circus, an almost infinite number of rings with exotic performers on stage 24 hours a day, 365 days a year. The circuses have become so ubiquitous that my wife and I, both to save time and to avoid saying *damn* too much in the presence of grandchildren, have condensed the **Rhett Retort** to an acronym: FMDIDGAD (pronounced, should you care to know, fum-did-ged.)

The circuses never leave town anymore, and the barkers pitching shows, the games along the midway, the peanuts and the popcorn never stop. Metaphorically speaking, posters announcing the performances are plastered everywhere, and our efforts to demand that others "post no bills" on our senses go ignored.

I am told by my TV that I should care who will get kicked off an island, who can or can't learn how to dance, or which person will prostitute him- or herself enough to get a rose from someone else who is seeking their fifteen minutes of fame by playing the clown in today's center ring. FMDIDGAD!

What is supposed to be news would try to interest me in the latest, often illegal and certainly ill-advised, antics of some rich TWIT (teenaged and witless). Many of these TWITs are no longer teenagers and no longer have the excuse that their frontal lobes are underdeveloped. FMDIDGAD!

My Internet browser would have me follow the most popular links of the day, though after looking at them, I realize that many relate to people who are high on my list of the most irrelevant people in the world. Of course, I don't really have such a list; creating it would simply be another distraction. FMDIDGAD!

Most amazing to me are the ongoing invitations from people about whom I know nothing and care even less to join clueless crowds that follow them on Facebook. Others want to tell me, in 140 characters or less, what they had for breakfast or that they are now walking off the stage (I can't get rid of them even when the lights go out and the show is supposedly over). I'm not anti-Internet—I've made a good living thanks in large part to the Internet. I'm not anti-television (I am related to that Farnsworth who invented it) or anti-news or even anti-celebrity (I'm quoting Clark Gabel after all). What I am opposed to is the ridiculous, the useless, and the inane—and the current inescapable ubiquity of the trivial. FMDIDGAD!

As with many of my other tags, the **Rhett Retort** has its flip side. I can, of course, post to my "wall" or "tweet" distractions to countless millions if they are willing recipients. I won't, but should the temptation arise, I grant the world every right to turn the **Rhett Retort** back on me, and even change one word: "Frankly, my David, I don't give a damn."

Now, to the truly dark side of distraction. I recognize a danger in my broad and sometimes flippant use of FMDIDGAD. I have a couple of pre-teen granddaughters. How will I assure that the TWITs who are so meaningless to me don't become more than a distraction and wield undue influence in their lives? To that extent, these circus clowns move not only into my circle of concern, but I must find a way to bring *their* ability to influence into *my* circle of influence. On a more macro scale, I recognize the damage that may be done if some rich impresario or ringmaster uses center stage to achieve political power; then what is now a mere distraction becomes a danger. These possibilities become and remain an allowed distraction, but for the most part I hope I can recognize the clowns for the distraction that they are and, without much thought, retort, "FMDIDGAD!"

The **Rett Retort** Restatement: There is much in the world that is trying to force its way into a potential and potent circle of distraction. These matters range from a serious hobby or avocation to TWIT disturbances. Evaluate the demands, opportunities, and input bombarding your life, and decide what and how much of it can be ignored.

CHAPTER 18

The Rattlesnake Wrongheadedness

A youth group from my neighborhood decided to take a deep-desert hike (not difficult as the deep desert is just an hour away). Their adventure took a serious turn, however, when one of the young ladies annoyed a rattlesnake and was bitten on the ankle. This happened in the old days before cell phones, so they couldn't call for help. The proper action would have been to rush the girl to the nearest hospital, about half an hour away, where she could receive antivenin and any other necessary treatment. Unfortunately, whether out of lust for revenge or a mistaken belief that they needed to have the snake so the doctors could identify it, the group chose to chase, capture, and kill the viper first. Leaving one person with the injured girl, they went on that quest and eventually succeeded. Then they headed to the hospital, forty-five minutes later than if they had ignored the cause and rushed for the cure. The young lady didn't die, but because of the delay, the venom damaged the blood vessels in her lower leg to the extent that they clotted irreparably, and she lost that leg at the knee.

I experienced similar wrongheadedness once when I was among the first on the scene of a serious accident. The young man involved had not noticed that the car in front of him had done an emergency stop until too late; he braked his motorcycle and went into a "head over," flying headfirst over the handlebars when his body didn't stop as fast as the bike. He hit the pavement, and the bike skidded into the next lane. As I reached the young man, he raised his head and began to struggle to get up, despite a concussion. "My bike," he whispered, "I have to see that my bike is okay." For some reason he was more concerned about his property than his life. We had to hold him down to keep him away from that motorcycle.

I have seen similar wrongheadedness applied to priorities not only in the midst of a crises but even as people prepared for a possible one. I was once engaged in crisis-preparedness and disaster-recovery discussions with a client. A major concern was that the client's primary facility was in a floodplain just below two significant reservoirs that were, in turn, on fault lines. If an earthquake breached either dam, their offices would be deluged by a wall of water higher than the three-story building that housed them. The discussion moved through apparently increasingly serious questions: Do we have the correct contact information for local emergency authorities? Are our systems properly backed up in a remote facility? How will we deal with the press if we are unable to meet the needs of our customers? How will we deal with the customers? What will the effect on our share value be? Will we be subject to business judgment questions for locating our offices in a floodplain in the first place? The conversation focused on increasingly horrible horribles in a long and fearsome parade.

After about an hour and a half of serious discussion, one of the members of the group who had been silent until then piped up: "Guys, all of what we are discussing is certainly serious, but shouldn't our first priority be making sure that the 650 people who work here make it to higher ground before they drown or are all killed by collapsing buildings?" There was a long, pregnant pause as everyone digested the basic fact that, value of life aside (and yes, we did value it), the company could not continue to exist without its people.

A crisis that leads to mistaken priorities doesn't always occur in an instant, like a snakebite, an accident, or an earthquake. One of the most sadly amusing legal cases I watched during my career turned on a crisis that had been years in creation. A local couple had worked hard together to build a very successful business valued, at the time one sued the other for divorce, at over 600 million dollars. In fact, they actually received an offer for that amount early in the proceedings. However, their hatred for each other and their dispute about who had created, and therefore deserved, more of the value that would result from an eventual sale blocked any hope of making that deal. As they fought and feuded, the business began to fail. Finally, after years of hearings, pleadings, and bitter disputes, the judge ordered the business sold. Deal value: less than half the previous offer. Their efforts to "get even" had cost each of the former marriage partners more than 150 million dollars. They had failed to recognize that their business was a different partnership than their marriage and had not prepared for its dissolution.

A crisis, of course, can awaken a whole slew of emotions: doubt, fear, anger, hatred. Unfortunately, it is the characteristics that lead to rational behavior that are most likely lacking: confidence, trust, calm, love, generosity. This makes the **Rattlesnake Wrongheadedness** one of my most important situation tags. Having a concrete plan in place that immediately resolves risks to flesh and blood and overrides discussions of cause, blame, and next-quarter earnings is crucial.

If you have read the **Second Opinion Requirement** and the **Rifle/Musket Conflict**, you know I am a deliberate person. In a crisis, however, while level heads must prevail, they must be heads that quickly recognize and resolve immediate priorities. I am a rifleman, not a musketeer, and I believe in getting a long-term memory consult. I am also a person who, just in case, always knows where the nearest exit is and how to get the most people through it if the alarm goes off.

The **Rattlesnake Wrongheadedness** Restatement: In a crisis, shift priorities to managing issues of immediate risk to life and limb and away from discussions of blame, cause, or property. Have a plan in place before the heightened emotions that accompany a crisis arise.

CHAPTER 19

The Earbudization Concern

During a recent layover at a major international airport, I sought out a quiet corner where I could read, work, and possibly relax a moment amid the hubbub. I settled into a corner seat and began to read some mindless novel, but after a few pages my attention was drawn to three teenage girls in school uniforms who had come into the area, also apparently seeking a little solitude. I noticed them in part because each was "earbudized," snugly plugged into digital audio players suspended around their necks. Each was also carrying a cell phone. They chose seats facing each other and soon were texting away. I continued to watch for a moment; analyzing people in public places is one of my favorite pastimes. From their body language and occasional simultaneous laughter, it didn't take long to discern something that brought me up short. There, within three feet of one another and in a relatively quiet place where conversation would have been comfortable, they were texting each other.

I admit I was more sad than surprised. This multitasking that allowed "conversation" while each tuned in to her favorite music isn't uncommon. What was sad was what their multitasking meant they were missing: dedicated commitment to a moment among real, not virtual, friends.

I had experienced similar feelings earlier in the same trip. I had watched a group of tourists board the train that would take them from Heathrow to London. Almost everyone in the group, old and young alike, settled their luggage, then themselves, and, as we began to move through the English countryside, budded up and devoted total attention to the screen of whatever they had plugged into. Why, I wondered, does someone fly thousands of miles to get out into the real world and then ignore it by disappearing into a virtual one that is available anywhere at any time?

A third incident made me more angry than sad. I had taken Roger to Beijing to transition a project that, after a corporate reorganization, now fell under his division. It was his first visit to Beijing, and he had expressed great interest in both the place and the project. As we taxied back and forth across the city from meeting to meeting though, he fell into a predictable pattern. He was attentive and an active participant during the meetings, but as soon as a meeting broke up, he pulled out his Blackberry and returned to his virtual office, sometimes remaining there for a forty-five-minute taxi ride that took him past most of what is famous about Beijing.

It was all I could do not to 'Gibbs' him. (For those of you who don't watch *NCIS*, to 'Gibbs' someone is to smack them in the back of the head to bring their attention back to the immediate issue.) For me, knowing the complexities and difficulties of dealing with life and business in China and with the Chinese, every moment I could spend in their world, watching how they worked, lived, and ate; what they bought and sold; and how they interacted, was a gift that would help me better accomplish what I was there for. Besides, Tiananmen Square, the Forbidden City, and the remnants of the Olympics were just plain worth a look. Roger, however, chose the virtual world over the real one pulsing with life around us.

Earbudized: to be plugged into a virtual world, more or, increasingly, less of one's own making, with the result of being isolated from the more real world that you are choosing or being compelled to ignore.

Earbudization is not just a problem for travelers. The executive admin to the CEO of a company I frequently visit would inevitably bud herself away as soon as she reached her desk and would stay there all day if she wasn't disturbed. I found it frustrating that when I went to visit her boss and needed to get her attention, I would have to knock loudly on her desk. I forbid my employees from "budding in" during working hours, mean and uncaring boss that I am.

In one company where I consulted, the various operating groups were seated in open-floor-plan configurations carefully designed to maximize intra-group communication and cooperation. However, I noticed on a number of visits that each group had members who plugged themselves into their virtual world so completely that another member of the group could have died loudly, and their passing wouldn't have been noticed until the end of the day (or at least until lunch, virtual food not yet being fully satisfying).

I am not a Luddite. I worked at the leading edge of technology, for companies that helped lay the groundwork for virtual worlds, including a very successful social-networking community created more than a decade before Facebook. I appreciate being able to video conference with colleagues in San Francisco, London, and Australia despite each of us being in a different time zone, bringing a closeness that used to require days of travel and tens of thousands of dollars in expense. I am, however, amazed, bemused, and troubled by reports that some video conferences are now attended by avatars. Gone are the days when the novelist can write "the tension in the room was palpable." Nowadays I wouldn't be surprised to read that "the virtual tension in the virtual room was virtually undetectable."

The problem of virtual isolation is, of course, not new. I confessed in the **Rikki-Tikki-Tavi Imperative** to occasionally being "libraryized" as a boy. Treatment (nowadays it might be called an "intervention") usually involved my parents pulling a book away from my face and forcing me out of doors and into contact with real people instead of the Hardy Boys or Leatherstocking. And we have, over time, been Zenithized, Atariized, Walkmanized, and so on. My fear, however, is that the path to personal isolation has never been so broad and easy as it is now, and it is getting broader and easier each day.

Some years ago the concept of managing by wandering around was in vogue, and I eagerly adopted my own version of it. As general counsel to increasingly large companies, I made it a practice to physically see every vice president and most directors and managers frequently. Scheduled visits at remote offices of one company would start with a formal discussion of an agenda I had sent in advance. That agenda covered the "important" matters that would keep the company legally safe. However, I soon learned that after the agenda was exhausted and we had relaxed into casual conversation, matters would surface that were likely much more important than the ones I had outlined.

At a company I worked for recently, the campus consisted of two large buildings. At least once a week I would wander every hall of both, and on almost every occasion someone would leave their computer—often having to de-bud first—and say, "Wow, you came by at just the right moment. I need to . . ." and we would have an important, and sometimes crucial, conversation.

I was not at all surprised when I read a study recently that determined that a person's influence in an organization is directly proportional to the amount of real "face time" they spend with their colleagues. A sub-finding was that the person whose office was closest to the entrance of an area, and therefore the one who more people had contact with simply as a result of passing by, was more connected and more influential than the guy at the end of the corridor. This study led me to wonder, even more than I already had, why we would earbudize ourselves into an isolation that makes us each a virtual "guy at the end of the corridor"?

The **Earbudization Crisis** Query: Do you evaluate the consequences of and amount of time spent in a virtual world, and do you balance it with your presence in the real world, inviting others as necessary to join you there?

CHAPTER 20

The Weed Ambiguity

I live in a beautiful sub-rural neighborhood, a "zoned for horses" piece of an otherwise megalopolis. I frankly don't particularly like or want horses, but my neighbor does. As a result, I live across the street from a well-kept and refreshingly green and unspoiled meadow. There across the street, plants in this pasture create a relaxing, natural addition to the view from my property, not to mention good fodder for horses. Trouble is, almost everything that grows in that meadow I consider a weed when I find it in my flower beds, and I go to considerable effort to remove it or prevent it from growing there.

I hire a local high school student to dig and care for my flowers and remove weeds. Trouble is, though a straight-A student and remarkable football player, he recently removed a bed of mint that I had just planted. For all his smarts and athleticism, he's not fully versed yet in what is or isn't a weed.

I once used this ambiguity about what constitutes a weed to my benefit. I lived in a community with very high ecological standards, which in general I applauded. Part of the city code protected any tree with a trunk diameter of more than four inches. At some point prior to my moving into my home, a careless breeze had blown a seed from a fast-growing tree into one of the flower beds. The prior owner had been less than fastidious about what he let prosper in his garden, and in due course that seed became a tree with a trunk now protected by law. This tree was unquestionably in a wrong place, threatening both the roof and the foundation, as well as shading out what I thought were more desirable plants. Not wanting to take the time and energy to get a variance to remove my nuisance, I looked for a shortcut. The same code that protected trees required property owners to keep their property clear of weeds. The definition of weeds included terminology such as "not purposefully planted," "unsightly," and "plants not in keeping with the tone of the town." My way was clear, and without a second thought, I declared the tree a weed and cut it down. I don't know what the town council would have done had they noticed my violence against one part of their code in favor of another, but I felt justified in my interpretation. The event did, however, give me philosophic pause and led me to this tag.

The weed metaphor is a common one; we use it to describe getting rid of something unwanted in the phrase "weed out." But are we adequately aware of the ambiguity surrounding just what is, or isn't, a weed? A plant in one place or context is a flower; in another place, it's a pest. A plant praised for its beauty may, if misused, be deadly (I'd wager that most suburban yards harbor at least one carefully cared for danger).

One context where to weed or not to weed has become abundantly clear to me is in connection with my love of books. While reading a book on books, I came across a description of a series published on U.S. history titled *Rivers of America*. The publisher had asked well-known authors and artists to consider the nation's history relating to America's great rivers that provided water, a means of transport, and often borders as the country developed. A volume on each of these rivers was written and published. I purchased and read a couple and, finding them both good literature and a rich source of Americana, decided to collect the whole set.

Acquiring the collection turned out to be much easier than I had expected. I simply found them at used-book sites on the Internet. I quickly learned that the most common, and usually least expensive, editions (even though most of what I bought were "first edition") were "ex library." These books had been acquired in the '40s, '50s and '60s by almost every public library in the country as "must haves." Now they were being weeded out. As I purchased each volume, part of my anticipation while I awaited its arrival was wondering which library it had come from. Who was now missing what was to me an exquisite opportunity to see U.S. history from a fascinating perspective? Their weeds, my garden.

The saddest applications of "weeding out" target human beings. It seems that an almost mandatory part of people management, particularly in large companies, is the annual weeding out of employees deemed "less productive." I watched what happened to Helen, an attorney with great transactional skills and entrepreneurial acumen as the company she served matured and then went public. The emphasis for the legal department shifted from minding the business to minding the regulations that plague public companies. I believe that management was inattentive rather than intentionally mean as Helen became, in the minds of the bean counters, not the productive asset that had helped create the company and its value, but a weed to be removed. It may be true that she was no longer the best fit for her prior role at the company, but perhaps management should have more horticultural training. Train, transplant, prune before you decide a productive vine is a weed.

The **Weed Ambiguity** Restatement: The value of an object is defined to a great extent by where it is and its usefulness in that context. A change of context results in a change of value, which means that a change in context may be a better value proposition than simply getting rid of something—or someone. No human being is a weed.

CHAPTER 21

The Oliver Twist

If you ask for a quote from the writings of Charles Dickens, you usually get one of two responses: Tiny Tim's "God bless us, everyone." from *A Christmas Carol* or *"Please sir, I want some more."* from *Oliver Twist.* You do get the occasional "It was the best of times, it was the worst of times . . ." but that's another story. It's the Oliver Twist line that I have chosen for an often-used tag.

The allocation of resources, plentiful or scarce, fair or unfair, is certainly one of the most complex issues in organizational behavior. This applies to families, companies, or orphaned inmates of poorhouses. To be sure, Oliver probably needed more, but the problem confronting the master of the poorhouse was that if he gave Oliver more, he would have to give everyone more, meaning there would be less for him to pilfer. We also often forget that Oliver was put up to making the demand as the result of a conspiracy; he got the short straw.

The **Oliver Twist** tag brings to mind what I have learned about resource allocation each time the situation arises. There is, indeed, a twist in this tag: there is a difference between wants, what Oliver wants, and needs, what Mister Bumble and the poorhouse board think the orphans need (and the fact that they want to keep the difference). Unfortunately, often it is "them that wants who gets and them that needs what go without."

My friend Tom told me how he achieved what he was told was the highest rating ever given on part of the U.S. Foreign Service exam. The section of the exam was a live group-interaction exercise. Each member of the group was given a scenario in which they were the head of a division of a State Department organization. They were told that there was a limited amount of money available to increase funding for the programs that their respective divisions supported, and each of them was to present, based on the documents they had been given, their best case to receive new funding. After a short time to prepare, they began to work through the group. It was a group of smart, eloquent people, and each made great arguments in favor of receiving the funds. When Tom's turn came, however, he gave a very short presentation that put the whole group into confusion and, I believe, to a degree of shame. He said, "As I have looked at the various programs under consideration here and evaluated the needs they raise compared to the needs raised by mine, it is clear that my program is significantly less critical than (and he named several of the others), and I therefore pass on receiving any budget increase." It was, apparently, the first time in the long history of the examination that anyone had responded by evaluating the needs of the whole rather than the wants of their own organization. How shocking it must have been to hear, "Please sir, I don't want anything. Give it to someone else."

I learned the difference between wants and needs from my father, who was a child of the Great Depression. Despite being an eight-member family headed by a woefully underpaid English professor, we never wanted. Dad succeeded in taking us around the world as a family, pausing to live for two years in the Middle East. That experience radically influenced our lives far more than a bigger house, a nicer car, or more "toys" ever could have. We all obtained graduate and/or postgraduate degrees with little or no debt. We worked our way through college, to a greater or lesser degree, depending on what portion of our expenses wasn't covered by the scholarships he encouraged us to earn through working for good grades. While I write this, Dad, at ninety-two, is a comfortably wealthy man.

The ultimate twist for me, and I use this tag to remind me of the fact, is that he who can do the most with the least wins. Accomplishment through better management rather than more resources really wins points with the Mr. Bumbles of the business world. As an added benefit, doing with less keeps you from getting talked into being the one who asks for more in a resource-constrained environment—and winding up apprenticed, like Oliver, to an undertaker.

And what about the other side of the **Oliver Twist**, the side dispensing the goods? Imagine a subordinate (or a child), even a favorite one, standing across your desk. You watch her mouth begin to form the words, and already the defenses go up. Are there many words more grating than "I want . . . I want . . . I want?"

There's one more lesson to be learned from Oliver's request. Dickens was serious in suggesting that Oliver and his hungry companions in the poorhouse both needed and deserved more and better, and he was hoping to make England and the world aware of the imbalanced allocation of resources that marked his society and continues to mar ours. So I have added the **Price of Tea in China** corollary to the **Oliver Twist**.

When I was growing up, when someone brought up something that we thought was irrelevant, a common response was, "And what does that have to do with the price of tea in China?" Frankly, I thought that very little I did or could possibly do would ever affect the price of tea in China. However, at the age of ten, my point of view was radically altered when I visited China, at least the New Territories. This was an area on the mainland that was politically attached to Hong Kong and under British control. It was, at the time, peopled by refugees from the People's Republic of China, and they were living in squalor. Multiple families were semi-sheltered from torrential rains in a shared cardboard shack. At that age, I understood neither the politics nor the macroeconomics that drove these people from their homes into those shacks, but I did begin to understand that something had certainly changed for these people and for the world; something had indeed affected the price of tea in China.

My understanding of those issues was enhanced when, during that same trip, I visited both India and England—India, where they were growing teas still called by Chinese names but no longer purchased from China for political reasons; and England, where they cheerfully drank their inexpensive tea picked by Indian Olivers who, I had seen, were very much justified in asking, "Please sir, I want some more."

It was much later that I learned about the true complexities of global interdependence, that what I am willing to pay for a gallon of gas in Utah may be the butterfly wings that determine whether an Indian farmer can afford to harvest his tea in a way that will allow it to remain competitive with teas that may be sold from China. Chaos theory would have me believe that, in fact, I can do very little that does *not* affect the price of tea in China.

The **Oliver Twist** Restatement: Constantly evaluate your need for resources. If you can do more with less, you win. Every use of a resource by you affects the value of that resource and its availability or unavailability to others.

CHAPTER 22

The Man with the Stamp Perplexity

During the part of my career when I was heavily engaged in government-relations work, I got to know, as a matter of course, others doing similar work. Also as a matter of course, when we got together, we would begin to exchange war stories, each trying to top the others in describing the bureaucratic boondoggles that plagued our efforts.

One of my favorite stories came from Mark, who had for years been trying to obtain a concession for his company in a third-world, Mediterranean country. After endless rounds of pleading, visits, and calls, he had been able to make an appointment for the CEO of his client with the minister of the department responsible for granting the concession. He accompanied the CEO to the meeting with great expectations, and to his delight, the discussion seemed to go exactly as planned. The minister was encouraging and supportive, and it appeared that the concession was within his client's grasp. After about an hour, everyone shook hands and left with promises and smiles on their lips. As they descended the stairs in front of the ministry building where the meeting had been held, the CEO and minister went on ahead, still exchanging pleasantries. Mark dropped back to discuss the concession and prospect of results with the minister's assistant, who had been in the meeting and to whom he owed much for setting it up.

"That was a great meeting. Thank you so much for helping me arrange it," Mark said. Then, with some trepidation, "What do you feel we accomplished?" The bombshell dropped.

"Nothing at all," the assistant responded.

As my friend looked at him in shock, the man went on to explain that although the concession did indeed fall under the purview of the minister they had just met with, the minister, an elected official, was from a different party than, and at cross-purposes with, the professional bureaucrats he managed. The concession would have to be processed and issued by those bureaucrats, and there was no way the minister was going to antagonize them by trying to force this particular position to a successful conclusion. The minister simply had no power to give what my friend had spent so much time and so much effort to obtain.

The **Man with the Stamp**. In much of the world, official action is still accompanied by someone taking a rubber, stone, or metal stamp; hitting an ink pad; and "pow," something suddenly becomes official. We cross borders, get building permits, obtain visas, even check out books (yes, there are people who still get paper books from libraries) to the sound of the man with the stamp.

In some cultures, the bureaucracy of the stamp is, figuratively and literally, a fine art. In China, the stamp, or chop, still replaces signatures, and having a beautiful chop is part of the game. There, the issue is not only finding the right person to "chop" everything you need to get done but also to get each chop in the right order. I have seen documents requiring ten chops before what to me was a simple matter could move forward.

My most frustrating **Man with the Stamp** experiences arose during the rather long period when I was trying to get things done in the former Soviet Union. It was relatively easy to get meetings with the agencies I had to deal with, but making progress was a nightmare. The Soviets had a double bureaucracy, the government side and the party side. In a negotiation meeting, you would enter the room and be seated at a table arranged with a clear "head" position. What I soon learned after so many meetings followed by no progress was that the person at the head of the table who did most of the talking was never the person who had the real authority to give me what I needed.

The real "man with the stamp" was a party official hidden among the others in the room, often in the guise of a note-taking secretary. The game became to see how quickly I could identify who really had the power and through their body language or occasional comment, determine if I was getting through to them. Then came the long process of getting everyone around them to let your matter pass up, down, or across the chain of command until it got done. Occasionally, after a meeting was over, I succumbed to the temptation of walking up to the person I had determined to be the real authority and thanking them profusely for their generous efforts to help me. This was sometimes met with icy silence, but more often it broke the ice and did move things along.

Perhaps one of the most frightening aspects of the **Man with the Stamp Perplexity** is seeing it come into play in a situation where the rule of law has broken down entirely (or never existed). I remember sitting with a client whose general counsel, as the meeting began, asked me to explain in detail the laws surrounding the process we were about to undertake. I admit, to my embarrassment, that I broke out in hearty laughter. The general counsel was indignant. Regaining my self-control, I apologized and explained that while I would be happy to explain the law of the jurisdiction on the matter, the law was irrelevant. While we would not break the law, our mission would be accomplished by understanding not the law, but the bureaucracy through which we would fight our way to the man with the stamp and convince him (or, occasionally but not often, her) that our cause was just and we should get the permits we needed.

Of course, you don't need to go to exotic places to be confronted by the man with the stamp. Who hasn't tried to get past a protective executive admin or even a doorman who, whether appropriately using or simply abusing their authority, tries to keep us from our objective. Even closer to home, a child knows which parent is the "man with the stamp" for a particular type of permission. Or, all else failing, how to wait for both to be gone and get permission from Grandma. "Pow!"

The **Man with the Stamp Perplexity** Restatement: Much of the power in the political world—and often in commercial, educational, and other organizations—is wielded by midlevel bureaucrats. These bureaucrats may operate outside the control of those who appear to, and perhaps legally should, have authority. Work is accomplished by finding, motivating, and obtaining appropriate action from the people who really can get the job done.

CHAPTER 23

The Chinese Water Torture Process

I was somewhat reluctant to include this tag under the name I use for it for fear it may appear to be an ethnic slur. However, after confirming that what I am about to describe truly has that title, but that in fact it has no proven roots in China, here goes.

I remember well that as children playing cops against robbers, cowboys against Indians, and so on, one of the worst threats we could use on a captured opponent was, "Now I am going to use the Chinese water torture." I don't recall ever doing it, most likely because it was difficult to restrain the captor long or well enough to put it into effect.

For those who didn't play such games or make such threats to your imagined enemies, Chinese water torture is a milder form of what we now call water boarding. The subject is completely restrained, and by use of a container with a small hole in it, water is dripped—drop, drop, drop—incessantly onto the victim's forehead. As I said, I can find no evidence that it either originated or was ever used in China, but it does appear to have been a common tool of the Spanish Inquisition. The result, as described by some who have used or experienced it, is a sense that a hole is being drilled through the head, accompanied by a corresponding degree of terror. Now, to the use of the tag.

For a significant part of the first fifteen years of my career, I was heavily engaged in government relations, commonly known as lobbying. I quickly learned that getting a permission, license, or some obstacle removed mostly involved convincing an official to do his or her job (or to at least get out of the way while another person did it). I also learned that the most effective way to do this was to follow what I soon tagged as the **Chinese Water Torture Process:** drop in, drop in, drop in; that is, frequent, in-person, face-to-face contact. After a few years of experience, I became quite adept at guessing how many "drop-ins" it would take to solve a particular issue, depending on its complexity and the nature of the bureaucracy involved. Letters, faxes, and later emails, while helping to keep the matter in the mind of the official involved, did not really do much to move issues toward resolution. I had to be there. I also learned that, generally, the frequency of the drop-ins didn't matter. If the issue was a twelve-visit one, it could be once a week for twelve weeks or once a month for twelve months. While it was true that visits that were too close or too dispersed resulted in increased resistance or lost momentum, within reason the frequency rule applied. And in many cases, there *was* an element of torture to those visits, both for the visitor and the visited. Bureaucrats don't want to be bothered, but that is part of the point. Eventually that bureaucrat who doesn't want to be bothered may give you what you want in part to avoid the next visit.

Convincing my clients of this reality was sometimes difficult. When the problem was in West Africa and my office in Europe, the time and travel expenses for a twelve-visit problem became considerable. (Though I did get more efficient with experience; eight-visit problems became six-visit problems and so on.) I spent a good deal of time convincing my bosses and the bean counters that my approach was the most efficient one. I pointed out that I needed x visits to create relationships, y visits to train the objects of the visit in their jobs so they became convinced that they could accomplish what I needed, and z visits to help them actually move the project to completion.

In one company my efforts to sell management on my approach were helped by the negative example of Heinz. He ran another division that had responsibilities for the same geography but another area of operation. He was officiously "efficient" in his operations. Heinz would plan his whole year's travel at the beginning of the year, budget accordingly, and stick to his plan like superglue. Unfortunately, he had not learned the **Chinese Water Torture Process** and grossly underestimated the number of drop-ins required. By the time it became apparent that his group was not making sufficient progress, because of time and budget limitations he had lost the flexibility to make the extra visits required. His failure, while unfortunate for the organization, bolstered arguments for my approach.

Heinz's approach emphasizes a **Chinese Water Torture Process** sub-rule as well: not only must you drop in the required number of times, but the visits must be long enough to make the progress planned for a particular trip. His hatred for "wasted time" led him to schedule flights that had him walking out of meetings just when progress was about to be made. He would arrive home having "done" everything he had planned but having accomplished little. He hadn't learned that dropping in may mean a very uncomfortable three days in a place where no one wants to be just to spend the right three minutes with the right person (see the **Man with the Stamp Perplexity**).

A second sub-rule worth mentioning I call the **Mop Up the Water Rule**. The **Chinese Water Torture Process** can, as I pointed out, leave both the visitor and the person visited feeling tortured. Once the objective of the visits is reached, friendly, "purposeless" attention may be required to maintain the relationship, and hopefully create a friendship, to be sure that progress made doesn't go down the drain with the metaphorical water used in the process.

I can't leave the **Chinese Water Torture Process** without visiting its negative corollary, the **Enlist the Dead Presidents Temptation**. Under very real pressure to accelerate the relationship, training, and handholding processes I have described, the question of whether there is another way raises its alluring head. Can't we buy progress? Payoffs, kickbacks, bribes, whatever name we use, are a real temptation. However, besides being nearly universally illegal, the **Enlist the Dead Presidents** approach is fraught with peril. Are you paying the right person? Will you get caught? Will he get caught? Do you really want to be a sleazy scumbag? I have been invited fairly frequently to lecture on international business processes, and the question of bribery invariably comes up. My response is always unequivocally negative, and it's not just because I believe in being law-abiding and honest. Bribery shifts the basis of power, leaving you heavily and permanently in debt to the other scumbag who will always be on the lookout for the next pound of flesh, and no one will be there to deny him the blood as well.

My own experiences, my experiences watching others who used the **Chinese Water Torture Process** well, and seeing the results from those who tried other means have taught me that the time and cost of frequent, face-to-face contact is worth every minute and penny. We end up not only getting the job done but can establish a long-term relationships based no longer on "torture," but on mutual understanding, respect, and, dare I say the word in the face of Facebook, real friendship!

The **Chinese Water Torture Process** Restatement: When your objective involves relationship building, carefully consider how much face-to-face contact is required; then commit to and make that contact despite the torture of repetitive visits and other costs. Alternatives involving payment for progress are not acceptable.

Tagging Tip: Experience is . . ? You can tag based on what you learn from others and avoid negative experiences you might otherwise not enjoy.

Who hasn't heard that "Experience is the best teacher"? While experience does have a way of lodging things solidly in our memory, how many of the learning experiences we remember most would we rather have avoided altogether? Often, learning through experience means a negative experience. Our educational system depends heavily on learning through the experience of others, through role-playing in a controlled environment, or on a micro level rather than in the harshness of the real world. To discover the reality that "an object in motion tends to stay in motion unless acted upon by force" with a rolling ball in physics class is preferable to learning that same law as we try to stop our car as it rolls away because we forgot to set the parking brake.

Furthermore, experience may *not* always be the best teacher. I remember reading a study in which two groups were taught to shoot basketball free throws. One group was given balls, sent onto the court, and after very basic instruction, allowed to practice. The other group was carefully instructed in the art and science of foul shooting and then allowed to watch the group that was actually practicing. After a number of hours, the practitioners and the theorists were pitted against each other to see who could make the most baskets in ten tries. In the study, the theorists outshot the practitioners.

I bring up the experience-theory dichotomy to point out that situation tags initially don't have to be based on personal experience. Tags based on education or the experience of others can allow us to be prepared to deal with a situation the first time we confront and recognize it. Many of the tags I describe, particularly those from my early life, are taken from the teachings or experiences of others, both real and fictional. Lifting a tag from a learned situation is absolutely legitimate, much like a warning sign that prevents us from driving off a cliff, even though we didn't post the sign ourselves. As we recognize and respond to tagged situations, experience reinforces and modifies, but it doesn't have to be the original source.

One of my most profound personal experiences in learning through "learning" rather than experience occurred when I visited St. Petersburg (then still Leningrad) with Dean. He was a professor of

Russian, and I was glad he was there to ask directions in this city where neither of us had been. One of our meetings was with Andre at his personal residence. Finding personal residences was difficult, in part because maps of the city were intentionally inaccurate to foil potential invaders from the West. We began by taking the metro to the general neighborhood where our Andre lived. As we came out of the metro station, Dean stopped dead, looked around, and said, "I've been here before."

I began to question his sanity. I knew very well that he had never been in the city, let alone that neighborhood. Meanwhile, he pointed out, accurately it turned out, the various features of the square we were standing in and the streets leading out of it. He then took off and I followed, more out of a desire not to be left alone than a belief that he knew what he was doing. After a short chase, he stopped. As I caught up with him, he pointed out that we had arrived at the apartment building we were looking for, without reference to any map, accurate or not. Laughing with a sort of amazed glee, my colleague explained. Quite by chance, the address we sought was near the residence of Raskolnikov, the fictional protagonist in Dostoevsky's *Crime and Punishment*. Dostoevsky had described the neighborhood so accurately in the novel that Dean, having read it tons of times preparing for classes, knew the neighborhood as if he had been there.

This experience with non-experienced education led me to adopt the **Leningrad Learning** tag. Thereafter, whenever possible, before going to a new place, I would read two or three classical novels set in that location. In the course of my work in more than seventy-five countries, this has been the best method I have found for preparing to deal with some of the physical and, more importantly, cultural realities of a new place.

The Sergeant York Strategy

At the age of ten I read a book of brief biographies of Medal of Honor winners. I suspect it was given to me by my paternal grandmother, who was always providing sources of moral encouragement. Frankly, I don't remember much of what I read, and nothing about what any of those honored did, with the exception of Sergeant Alvin York.

York was one you would hardly expect to become a Medal of Honor recipient. He was, in fact, a pacifist and had tried to avoid WWI altogether as a conscientious objector. But he eventually ended up just like millions of other men, in the trenches in France. He had, however, a talent that set him apart: he was an exceptionally good shot. It was this ability that allowed him to adopt the strategy that stuck so forcefully in my ten-year-old brain and became an early tag, before I even thought of tags as tags.

World War I was a war of trenches. The opposing forces established lines some distance from each other and dug long, deep trench fortifications. To make any progress, one side or the other would eventually leave the relative safety of their trench (usually after heavy artillery barrages) and advance toward their opponents' trenches. If they succeeded in reaching the other's trench, close-quarter combat would ensue. All in all, it was like a very deadly game of "steal the flag."

Imagine, if you can (and despite having visited those battlefields, I still find it hard to begin to comprehend the horror), looking over the edge of your trench and seeing waves of enemy soldiers moving across the intervening hundreds of yards toward you. The natural reaction would be to look straight ahead and shoot at the person closest to you; he was the greatest risk, the closest to entering your trench to bayonet or be bayoneted.

Under those very circumstances, Sergeant York had the calm, the cleverness, and the marksmanship to adopt a counterintuitive approach. This time, imagine you are the advancing force. As you leave your trench amid the roar and confusion of battle, your attention is locked on your comrades advancing in front of you. Suddenly, one of them and then another is hit by enemy fire. Your natural reaction is to duck for cover, conceal yourself in a shell crater, and continue your advance, if at all, by dodging from one point of cover to another. York's strategy recognized this propensity to duck and disappear if those in front of you go down. So he would fire first at the enemy farthest away in the advancing groups. As a result, the advancing line, not seeing anyone go down in front of them and believing the enemy fire to be ineffective, would continue their advance in the clear, rather from shell crater to shell crater.

Imagine again that you are almost to the enemy trenches, no one in front of you has fallen, and you believe you are a part of a successful charge. At the last moment you look around to your comrades at arms, and you suddenly discover that, literally, no one has your back and you are about to enter trenches full of your enemy essentially alone.

Sergeant York, though effective at dispatching the enemy, did not win the Medal of Honor for the number of men he killed. While in command of the small remnant of his company after the death of the officers, he used his strategy to get an attacking group much larger than his own to surrender, thus, in fact, saving rather than taking lives. And winning the Medal of Honor.

As I have observed organizational changes, some of which have created antagonisms bordering on warfare, I have noted a strong tendency to take the intuitive approach. A group reorganization almost always begins with the firing of one or more people at the top, taking out the guys in the front of the charge, which results in the rest of the group diving for cover. I have also seen very successful reorganizations that were done from the bottom up so that by the time the boss was fired and the new management stepped in, the whole was functioning better than before, and the group had "surrendered" to their new structure without the fear and resistance that results when such a reorganization begins with a, metaphorically speaking, bloody decapitation.

In transactional negotiations, the tendency is to create a list of issues and move through them, checking them off one by one without regard to importance or prioritization. On the other hand, I have been involved in deals where one side has carefully orchestrated the order of issue resolution so that by the time they reached the most difficult problem, the other side had conceded so much that there was no turning back, and "surrender" was inevitable.

Perhaps the circumstances most amenable to the **Sergeant York Strategy** are staff and committee meetings. I have worked on committees where the chair would call the meeting to order, adamantly state his or her position, and then proceed to shoot down anyone who raised any contrary point of view. In many cases, not only did the others present dive for the nearest cover, but it soon became clear to those of us who cared that we may as well not even leave our trenches. We had been blasted by the chair's cannonade but remained relatively unscathed from the attack. We changed neither our minds nor our positions, and no advance was made toward the real resolution of any issue.

On the other hand, I know, admire, and try to emulate a master at running committee or any other meetings. He would begin by stating only some of the issues to be addressed and then have each person present express their opinion or concerns, starting with the least-senior person. That way, each participant could contribute without contradicting any superior. By asking questions as the matter progressed, this chair succeeded in guiding the discussion in such a way that by the time all had contributed, a consensus had been reached and all he had to do was confirm it. Everyone had reached the chair's trench alive, but they still surrendered.

I have wondered in a much more modern context if the **Sergeant York Strategy** would succeed in our current war on terrorism. Our tendency, it seems to me, is to focus aggressively on taking out the leaders of dangerous organizations. I wonder if, rather than offering a $25 million reward for one leading person, it might be more effective to offer $100,000 rewards for 250 operators who, having, fewer resources to allow them to hide and a less loyal following, might be easier to catch. While I wouldn't expect a leader thus deprived of support to surrender, he certainly would find himself much less effective, having no support in the trenches.

The **Sergeant York Strategy** Restatement: When managing organizational change or trying to reach negotiated agreement, carefully consider the order in which changes should be made or issues resolved to minimize conflict and allow each decision to support those that remain to be made.

CHAPTER 25

The Puddle/Pond Dichotomy

A couple of years ago the state of Utah had a record water year. The snowpack in the Wasatch and Uinta mountains that feeds local lakes and reservoirs was 300 percent of normal in places. This was great news for Utahans because they have little rain in the summer. Whether the desert they live in is green or brown come July depends on how much winter water they can store. Whatever water they can't capture flows not into an ocean-bound river, as it does elsewhere on the continent, but into the Great Salt Lake. With this exceptionally wet winter, the water level of the Great Salt Lake rose 5 feet over a few months. Incredibly, this 5-foot rise in water level increased the surface area of the lake by more than 40 percent. The lake covered 1,200 square miles as the snow melt began, but after few weeks it covered over 1,700 square miles. Yet even with the 5 additional feet, because that water is spread over such a large area, the lake's average depth remained well under 20 feet.

Contrast this with Lake Baikal in Siberia. The surface area of that lake is 12,000 square miles, and it is 5,400 feet deep, filling a great canyon created by continental drift. Were it to receive the same amount of water that will lift the Great Salt Lake another 5 feet and increase its surface area by 40 percent, the change in Lake Baikal would be negligible.

At its new level, the Great Salt Lake once again reached the sailboat marina that for the past few years had been high and dry, and the federal bird refuge filled with water and once again became a stopping place for thousands of migrating fowl. However, as the next two water years were typical, the lake receded, the sailors lost their docks again, and the birds had to find refuge elsewhere. In short, the Great Salt Lake is a (very) big but shallow puddle, drying up in the hot sun unless it's replenished frequently. Lake Baikal in Siberia, however, is the world's largest fresh water pond, and its depth and surface area have changed little over thousands of years.

I illustrate the principle behind this tag to my Boy Scouts by taking two cups of water out to the parking lot. I pour one on the asphalt and set the other beside the puddle I've created. "Which," I ask, "looks more impressive?" A cup of water, well-spread, makes a big splash, and they generally respond by being impressed with the puddle. I bring them back half an hour later when the spill has evaporated and the glass of water is still almost full and ask them which they would rather have had if they were thirsty. They generally get the point. (I used to illustrate this with a flashbulb and a flashlight and ask which they would rather have on a dark night, but flashbulbs are now hard to come by. Oh, for the olden days.) Splash or flash, the lesson is the same: big or bright but short term, impressive but then gone; or smaller looking with less flash but there for the long term, reliable and functional beyond today.

Baseball offers another example. When I played back in my teenage years I wasn't particularly good. I did learn quickly that I could not hit the ball on the fly past the outfielders; for me to "go for the fence" was a wasted effort. That was why I seldom hit a fly. I would try for a base hit, low and into the outfield. Most of the guys I played with were of another mindset; they constantly tried to bash the ball as high and far as they could. One day, more by accident than intent, I connected and sent one way into right field. Unfortunately, it didn't quite make the fence, and the fielder was good enough to catch it. My being "out" notwithstanding, one of my teammates pounded me on the back and said, "Wow, Farnsworth! I didn't think you had that in you." I thanked him and then, uselessly it turned out, pointed out that despite the fantastic fly, I was out. I went on to explain, to an unappreciative audience whose eyes soon glazed over, that the most effective hit in baseball might be one that clears the infield a foot off the ground and hits the ground before reaching an outfielder. They didn't care. For them, it was go for the fence, the splash, the spectacular.

The choice between flashy or functional is not always easy. No doubt flash has its place. Entertainment relies on it. If I apply my baseball strategy to football, the reality is that a team that could move the ball 2.51 yards on every play, every time, would win every game. For a few games, their fans would be wild about their wins. However, soon no one would want to watch and we would have a Super Bowl winner that no one could love. In time, professional football would die from boredom. We watch baseball, football, racing, and most sports for the spectacular: the home run, the punt return for a touchdown, the crash into the wall. With entertainment, of course, comes entertainers, and our culture likes its entertainers to continue the splash and flash even after they leave the stage or screen, court or course. I have a hard time with that one. I may love to hear you sing, but that doesn't mean I want to know your political opinion or what you had for breakfast.

Entertainment is about splash and flash, the spectacular. In real life, however, the **Puddle/Pond Dichotomy** helps me maintain balance. When it comes to cars, homes, clothes, getting my job done, or real relationships, how much is flash, how much function? As I purchased a car recently, the salesperson pointed out all the nifty stuff that allowed him to charge me more and more for the same transportation value. Since my purpose was simply to get from point A to point B, all that stuff simply became more chances for something to break right after the end of the warranty period. He won—sort of. I bought the fancy car, accepting the flash as part of something I wanted otherwise.

The Great Salt Lake is an amazing body of water. It's even responsible for creating "The Greatest Snow on Earth" in the nearby ski resorts by pumping moisture into winter storms from the northwest. However, because of its erratic annual ebb and flow, it's not a reliable pond in the same way as, say, Lake Baikal. When I need to be sure of a drink of water, give me, please, a deeper, more constant source.

The **Puddle/Pool Dichotomy** Query: In a given situation, what is the balance between appearance and result in relation to an objective? Does this situation require a puddle or a pond? Are you being blinded by the flash?

CHAPTER 26

The Smokey the Bear Command

One of the few lessons I vividly remember from my early elementary education is anti-forest-fire training. Each spring for at least three years, we filed into an assembly and spent half an hour watching a film about that great preventer of forest fires, Smokey the Bear. This training was highly appropriate; I lived in a rural/suburban interface area with very dry summers, and we had at least one major fire a year, despite the training. However, what stuck with me from the assemblies, besides a catchy tune about Smokey that I can still sing and the admonition to never play with matches, is not the lesson about preventing forest fires. What I remember best is the advice that Smokey's mother supposedly gave her cub: "If danger threatens, climb a tree." The original Smokey was, in fact, rescued from high in a tree where he had survived a fast-moving forest fire. He was scorched and smoked but alive because he had climbed above the worst of the blaze. This admonition to flee danger, one continually reinforced by my own caring parents, became one of my first conscious situation tags.

Where we should draw the line between getting out of danger's path and courageously standing our ground is the complex question raised by this tag. Making the right choice between stand or flee, and the consequences accompanying the wrong choice, is a fundamental element of Judeo-Christian and other ethical philosophies. King David is a prime example. As a young man, he fought and slew Goliath, the enemy of his people. Later he was felled himself when he couldn't turn away from his lust for another man's wife. He should have followed the example of his predecessor in the Old Testament, Joseph.

Joseph, after being sold into slavery by his brothers, rose through his courageous efforts to become the manager of Potiphar's house. With this position of responsibility came contact with Potiphar's wife, who tried to seduce him. When she wouldn't take his oft-repeated "No" for an answer, Joseph took action, which is recorded in one of the most instructive verses in Hebraic scripture: "Joseph left ... and fled." He was fired, but by fleeing he survived to make it to the big time: just a few years later, he had gone from being ousted at Potipher's place to CEO of all of Egypt.

To flee—is it courage or cowardice? I was once one of two industry representatives invited to testify before a legislative committee concerning a law that, I remain convinced, was counterproductive, contrary to the interests of the state, and otherwise just plain stupid. It had, however, strong special-interest backing. I quickly learned, as I began to describe the "industry" position, that I had not been invited to the hearing to be listened to but rather to become a whipping boy that supporters of those interests could use to make their point before the press. As it became clear I would get nowhere with my presentation, I turned, looking for support from the other representative who was to testify following me, only to see him disappear through the back door. I was, at that moment, extremely put out (to put it politely) that he had "chickened out" on me. Later, however, I had to concede that his behavior was not only appropriate but intelligent. Seeing that we would get nowhere—and that this had been the plan all along—he had no reason to play into his enemies' hands and expose himself or the company he represented to the persecution that was waiting.

On another occasion, the willingness to press on in the face of danger by a colleague put us almost literally into the fire. Steve and I had been trying to negotiate concessions from a rather hostile government and had run into the proverbial brick wall. I had decided to spend the rest of our time in the country keeping a low profile and taking on the role of casual tourist as best I could until our flight the next day. Steve, on the other hand, true to his Type-A personality and unquenchable desire to get things done against all odds, wanted to make one more contact. His one more call set off a chain of events that set the process we were engaged in back several years and came close to landing us in jail.

I remember an old proverb I think I heard first in Danny Kaye's movie *The Court Jester:* "He who fights and runs away lives to fight another day." The line is spoken by the bad guy and is supposed to demonstrate that in spite of all his blustering about being thus and so, he is, in fact, a coward. However, cowardice aside, do we recognize when the moral, and possibly even the physical, high ground is actually somewhere else and that it may be wise for us to get there quickly?

We often hear Nietzsche's statement in this form (in fact, I heard it misquoted less than an hour ago): "That which doesn't kill me only serves to make me stronger." (Actually, the correct translation from German is "That which doesn't destroy me, strengthens.") An interesting point of view, and possibly true in some circumstances. However, getting past the first part, "Ay, there's the rub." What if it does destroy me? I won't be around to gain the added strength.

Just as social pressures have made it difficult to say no (see the **Bastogne Response**), increasing moral ambiguity as to what is or is not courage has made it difficult to contemplate fleeing in the face of danger. What remains important to me is that Smokey survived and became a symbol to remind us to avoid conflagrations (and Joseph became master of all Egypt) because he fled.

The **Smokey the Bear Command** Restatement: Understand and accept that there are situations when, in times of commercial, moral, or physical danger, the best response is to flee.

CHAPTER 27

The Perfection Paradox

A longtime friend is an architect of considerable renown. When we discuss her work, Sarah exudes confidence in her ability to please her clients while maintaining her creativity and artistic integrity. So I was surprised one day to walk into her office and find her scrunched over her drafting table with a look of doubt and worry furrowing her face. I asked with sincere concern what the problem was. She replied that she had been commissioned to design a church, and then she dropped the "P" bomb: "And because it is to honor God, I want it to be perfect."

I knew Sarah to be a woman of deep faith, and rather than enter into any discussion of the philosophical issues surrounding perfection, I simply mumbled my assurances that she could meet the task. I recognized, however, that she was straying deeply into the **Perfection Paradox**. It's said that the good is the enemy of the great, but to me the next step in that line of reasoning is that perfection is the enemy of everything. (I'm speaking of temporal perfection here, rather than the hope for spiritual perfection, which is faith's foundation and a different topic.) Some of the questions that rolled through my mind, and which I didn't put to my friend, were, "Perfect as an awe-inspiring edifice?""Perfect as a cozy place of worship?""Perfect as an engineered structure that would stand up to time, earthquake, and flood?" Sarah was so consumed with seeking perfection, that rather than at least approaching it in her design, she was, as she herself acknowledged, getting nowhere. She needed to satisfy herself with the excellence she attained in all her work and move on.

On another occasion, I was attending a continuing education seminar after being in legal practice long enough to have become pragmatic and, possibly, a little bit cynical. At one point in the discussion, a bright, young, just-out-of-school attorney sitting next to me piped up and said, "I want each of my clients to have the benefit of my best work; I want each of my efforts to be perfect." The gentleman on her other side, perhaps even a bit more cynical than I, spoke up and said with all kindness and sincerity, "Miss, most of your clients can't afford your best work, let alone perfection." We then proceeded to have a discussion about sufficiency (which, in my mind, still requires excellence) and how when one is paying another by the minute, the one paying is likely to have a different point of view on how close to perfection one needs to come to get the job done. The last 1 percent under the law of diminishing returns can come at an outrageous, and often pointless, cost.

But wait. Isn't that cost worth it when, for example, life is at risk? If you were going to be shot into space, you old cynic, wouldn't you want the spaceship to function perfectly? Not necessarily. What I would want, knowing that perfection in any physical system is nigh impossible, is sufficient redundancy to resolve any failure when something went wrong. I want solid functionality and serious backup. Functionality with high redundancy is not perfection, but it can deliver the same results. And it's much more doable in the real world where things really do go wrong.

Another part of the perfection paradox is, of course, that perfection is subjective. Think about what you meant the last time you said, "That's perfect." Didn't you really mean, "You have met my needs to the point that I have nothing to complain about and might even be willing to praise?" And might you admit that under other circumstances, or from another's point of view, things might be different?

You don't even have to agree that perfection is subjective; I have it on judicial authority. One of my clients used the word *perfect* in a product name and related advertising. A competitor sued us, claiming that the use of the word *perfect* with our product was comparative and disparaging. It implied that our product was better than theirs, and they demanded we quit using the word. The judge agreed that the word could be considered comparative but concluded that it couldn't be objectively defined because each person had his or her own opinion as to what it meant. Thus, our promotions became a subjective expression and resulted in what in advertising is called puffery; everyone knows nothing is perfect unless they personally think it is.

So, *perfect*? I hear the word and shudder. My mind begins to process. How much more will it cost? How much longer will it take? Perfect for what purpose, and who will decide when we get there? I may, with my architect friend, seek the perfect on some spiritual plane, but here on Earth, I will strive for, and be satisfied with, an appropriate degree of excellence.

The **Perfection Paradox** Query: When tempted by perfection, ask yourself: Am I delaying progress, increasing cost, or creating complexity or confusion because I am looking for "Perfection" in a process or result for which perfection is neither pertinent nor possible? Worse, am I putting off beginning because I'm afraid I won't reach the perfection I expect?

CHAPTER 28

The Italian Tax Code Conundrum

I spent a significant part of my career working in Europe for U.S.-based companies and traveled extensively throughout the continent. One reality of being an expatriate is that you meet other expatriates and share war stories. A particularly common topic of conversation was how we were treated by our respective employers, what our "expat package" looked like, which would lead to a "mine is better than yours" or "how can you live with that?" comparison.

I was required to visit Italy frequently, and I soon had a number of U.S. friends there. In one of those conversations comparing companies, the discussion turned to taxes, particularly how we and our companies dealt with personal income tax. Since we were usually employed by multiple companies in several countries at once, our tax situations were always complex.

My Italy-based friend Michael informed me that in order to demonstrate that they were "good citizens" in a place where they were considered "foreigners," his company insisted that he scrupulously conform with Italian tax law. This included paying a full personal income tax as required by law. His employer hired one of the big international accounting firms to prepare his tax returns to assure both him and themselves that his return and payment were completely correct and his status as an Italian taxpayer beyond reproach. The trouble was, after Michael's first full year in Italy, the accountants came to him with the startling news that in order to completely comply with the burdens placed on him by the various parts of the Italian tax code, he would be paying 105% of his income in taxes. My friend had fallen afoul of a common problem in complex systems and one that, in his honor, I now tag as the **Italian Tax Code Conundrum** (or "**ITCC**").

The **ITCC** arises from a very simple reality: Italians cheat on their taxes. Please don't think I am unfairly singling out the Italians. Tax evasion is a well-developed, worldwide science. It does appear, however, that the Italians, in part as a form of protest, are particularly artful practitioners—the Michelangelos of defrauding the Feds, we might say.

Tax evasion can take many forms: false returns, double sets of books, invoicing "errors." Since Italian property taxes are based on appraisals, owners of valuable properties intentionally let the exteriors decay while creating luxurious homes behind faded facades. They are conveniently not at home when the appraiser comes, so the value is judged by that exterior only. I learned that whole businesses are run "off the books." The city of Naples exported five million pairs of gloves one year and didn't have a single glove manufacturer on its tax rolls.

It is this almost compulsive dodging of tax liabilities that gave rise to my friend's dilemma of having his tax liability exceed his income. The conundrum arises in a relatively simple way. Italian agencies and entities at various levels each have their budgets, and related tax regulations are approved and tax rates set accordingly. Simple, right? Wrong. Because (almost) everyone fudges, there's a shortfall, and that shortfall is covered by another tax. Then the shortfall fix falls short because of additional fudging, so added to the income tax, which was augmented by the real-estate tax, we get a use tax and a license tax and a street tax and a luxury tax and on and on. Each tax is set to cure the shortfall of the others, but with the dodging that occurs in each category and at every level, tax rates that should equal 105% achieve a real collection rate of 40%. Each new tax is a work-around or patch to deal with the failure of a former change to solve the core issue: noncompliance.

After years in the software industry, I became acquainted with another example of patching followed by the patching of patches. When a problem is found in a software product, it is often solved by a "patch": Rather than rewriting the problem code, a bit of new code allows the problem to be bypassed. In fact, whole new features are often added through what are essentially massive patches. There is a degree of logic to this. It's difficult in a complex software product to know what the consequences will be of changing or removing current code when making changes or upgrades. The old code might be necessary for some operation that the developer is not aware of, so it is left in. After a few iterations, it is not uncommon for a significant percentage of the code in a software product to do nothing. It remains because no one is sure what would happen if it were removed. Patch is piled on top of patch, until it's unclear what is patch and what is the original fabric of the product.

Developers call what I have just described "code debt," and the term *debt* is a valid one. Each piece of unnecessary code left in eventually extracts a price. The product becomes slow, unwieldy, or prone to errors. New revisions become increasingly difficult because developers must take into account the potential effect of the old code. Old code doesn't allow the program to run within new operating systems. Eventually, the whole product must be rewritten at significant cost; the debt must be paid off.

To put this tag in a simpler, and probably more familiar, way, it is the "poor boy's bicycle" dilemma. When my bike tire goes flat, do I patch, and then patch on the patch, or do I splurge and pay the price for a new inner tube?

Whether seen from the macro level of the Italian fiscal system, the technical level of code debt, or, as I still remember well, the difficulty of making sure that a patch covers part of another patch on a worn bike tube, this tag helps me respond to situations I confront at work, at home, and in my personal activities.

When my division is failing to meet its objectives, do I simply need to move a few people around or work a few more hours myself, or do I need to stop and analyze the whole structure and then move toward a more difficult, long-term fix?

Do those yellow patches in the lawn mean spreading a little fertilizer here and there, or a complete treatment to kill whatever might be eating the roots of the grass?

Does resolving the occasional heart palpitations I feel after a stressful day require just one can of Coke less or a ten-minute walk at lunch more, or a total lifestyle change?

Most critical, will a temporary fix now result in increased future costs as each temporary solution simply delays an investment that must be made and will cost more in the future? Taking that ten-minute walk is certainly more pleasant than slowly recovering from a heart attack—or the alternative of not recovering at all.

Patch, repair, replace, reinvent. Where is the best return on my investment, and should I look long-term or be satisfied with a more immediate solution? To be sure, getting the Italians (or any society) to respect their tax code so that it can be single-layered and simple is not easy, but in the long run, putting patch on patch on patch may not be the quick-and-easy fix it once appeared to be.

The **Italian Tax Code Conundrum** Query: When addressing a problem, ask yourself; should I patch, with the likelihood that I will eventually have to solve the problem more permanently in the future, or should I solve for the long-term now?

CHAPTER 29

The Dumpster Dilemma

I collect historical firearms. A reality of this hobby is that I am dealing with used items, and much of what I want is in the hands of other collectors. The best "deals," therefore, arise when someone who doesn't find value in what I am looking for gets rid of it, and it ends up in the want ads or in a secondhand or "antique" store. The trouble is, when something of possible value ends up in a secondhand situation, you have to ask why it's there. Is it stolen? Is it fake? Is it broken or missing pieces or mismatched? (The teacup collector will ask the same questions.) Where an item is found affects the perception of its value. The shelves in secondhand shops are full of junk, so what I am looking at there, despite the ability I claim as a collector to know otherwise, just might be junk. I recently saw among the many used rifles on the shelf of a local shop a very nice piece that looked to be brand new. But I couldn't bring myself to buy it because it shouldn't have been there. I had this nagging sense that if someone was willing to part with it, there had to be something wrong with it. To get to the point of this situation tag, dumpsters are for garbage, and, therefore, I assume that anything that I find in one is likely to be garbage.

The hard and soft sciences have a more sophisticated name for this tag. While **Dumpster Dilemma** is easy to remember and describes the issue well, I favor the scientific tag every now and again because it sounds so cool: "Evaluation based on simultaneous presence." To the microbiologist, knowing that x is almost always seen in the presence of y may lead him to conclude that what he sees with y is x, even though x can't be separately identified. To the sociologist, or police officer for that matter, if teenager 1 is seen with teenagers 2 through 10, and teenagers 2 through 10 are members of gang Z, teenager 1 is a member of gang Z. Fair? Maybe not. A likely assessment? Yup. More on that later.

My work has recently brought me smack into the middle of big-budget advertising. A major dilemma that comes with advertising decisions is that ads have to appear somewhere—during or within a TV or radio show, on an Internet site, in a magazine, on a billboard, and so on. This means, however, that in every case, ads appear in a context. How will that context affect that advertisement and the overall value of the brand being presented? If I place an ad during Howard Stern's show, will I offend potential (or current) customers who think he is rude, offensive, or unintelligent and therefore weaken my message and brand? If I place an ad during Rush Limbaugh's show, will I offend those who feel that he is rude, offensive, or unintelligent?

A couple of Internet companies recently decided to engage in a cross-branded advertising campaign, with each placing ads and links on the sites of the other. This placement suggested that if a customer liked Brand A, they would probably like Brand B. However, the marketing team at Brand A was concerned, knowing that while Brand B could likely drive traffic and sales to their site, Brand B's less-than-stellar reputation could affect customer perception of their more respectable brand. Their fears were soon confirmed. Shortly after the campaign began, Brand A's customer-service group noticed a significant increase in calls about the product advertised, but more importantly, they began to get calls complaining about the quality of Brand B's product. Brand A quickly learned that the loss of brand value was not worth any increase in sales resulting from the relationship, and it was terminated. Note that even the most basic of Internet advertising agreements recognize the **Dumpster Dilemma** and don't allow the banners of reputable advertisers to appear on porn sites or sites that promote alcohol, tobacco, or other "disreputable" products. Further, high-brand-value sites don't allow products their customers or the general public may find offensive to be advertised on them.

As I have thought through the **Dumpster Dilemma** again, I realize that another common aphorism may fit here as a situation tag: "A man is judged by the company he keeps." I don't like that version. It's a statement of what often happens but often shouldn't. The **Dumpster Dilemma** tag reminds me that I should be careful with the reputation of brands, products, promotions, and myself. It also reminds me of the dangers of evaluations based on simultaneous presence. Mother Teresa's work in the slums of India made her a saint, not a slumdog. Not all Spanish Christians during the late Middle Ages were sadistic inquisitors, just as it is common knowledge that not all Muslims are terrorists.

You will be better at some things and worse at others than your neighbors, "the Joneses." Evaluation should be made on why something is where it is, not just on the where. Not everything you find in a dumpster is garbage just because some thoughtless, uncaring person put it there, just as everything in the Guggenheim is not art, just because some thoughtless, uncaring person (not really, just persons of different tastes) put it there.

The **Dumpster Dilemma** Restatement: In situations of association, recognize the temptation to evaluate based on simultaneous presence. Know, however, that brands, products, work, and people will be evaluated based on simultaneous presence, so appropriately protect those you have responsibility for against that reality. In your own judgments, look beyond the "dumpster" where something is found and evaluate on other appropriate criteria.

CHAPTER 30

The Third Law of Motion Denial

I have seen Newton's third law of motion expressed in many different ways, but for purposes of this tag I will use the simple definition that has stuck in my mind since I first heard it as a child: "For every action there is an equal and opposite reaction." One common way to illustrate this rule is to describe the very real result of the kick that accompanies firing a rifle. I have a target rifle that fires a bullet with a mass of 70 grains driven by a powder charge that launches that bullet at a velocity of 3,200 feet per second. The rifle itself has a mass of 70,000 grains. This means that in a frictionless vacuum, the bullet would move forward 3,200 feet in a second, and the rifle, having 1,000 times the mass, would move 3.2 feet in exactly the opposite direction during that same period. Since the rifle is resting on my shoulder, the force that moves the rifle meets resistance, and I feel a kick.

Of course, in the real world we don't experience frictionless vacuums. In fact, the bullet is experiencing the effects of the third law with every air molecule it meets. As it pushes them out of the way, they push back with equal force, and because that bullet is moving millions of molecules, their mass adds up and the bullet quickly slows.

There was a time when I wondered whether each tag I had developed and used could be described in terms of a natural law. While many could, the limitations were daunting. In fact, one of the major ones was that whole vacuum business. Natural laws as we define them often describe what happens in a frictionless vacuum or a frictionless, energy-less vacuum or even a frictionless, energy-less, gravitation-less vacuum. Human activity almost always confronts all of these: friction, energy, gravity, and gases as well (often in the form of hot air).

I also know that human endeavor allows for, and in my mind demands, constant, successful disruption of the third law. In describing the **Chaos Disclaimer** I noted that, except in the case of forces of nature beyond our control, we don't have to accept the consequences of sensitive dependence. We can react with what I called constant intelligent intervention. In **Escape Velocity** I spoke of BDRs, big dumb rockets. In fact, those rockets are not quite so dumb as the name implies. Rockets are very direct examples of the third law. As fuel burns with explosive energy in a combustion chamber, great force is exerted equally in all directions. Because some of that force escapes in one direction, the rocket flies off in the other direction. With no intervention, the rocket will fly in exactly the opposite direction to the force that is allowed to escape.

But back to the "not so dumb" part. When we launch a rocket with a purpose, such as reaching the space station, letting it fly off in a straight line wouldn't be the best way to get where we want to go. We would have to be sure that the space station was in exactly the right place when we ignited the rocket, that there were no wind, and so on. So rather than deal with potentially fine margins of error, we put the exhaust nozzle of the rocket on a gimbal, allowing us to redirect the "opposite" force and turn the rocket according to our will. The forces at work in our lives, those we create as well as those we are required to react to, including the actions of others and most natural events, present the same opportunity: we can direct our response, our reaction, according to our will.

Note that I did not say *free* will. Will and its expression are never free; in fact, expressing our will often comes at great expense and risk. Which brings us back to the **Third Law of Motion Denial**. That bullet and the rifle, the air molecules and my shoulder, they are all subject to natural law, but where I point the rifle, how I hold it to my shoulder, or whether I pull the trigger—or even load it at all—are subject to my will.

Metaphorically, the human equivalent of Newton's third law of motion is, if you punch me in the face and break my nose, then I will punch you back with equal force and break your nose. It's the eye-for-an-eye, tooth–for-a-tooth rule. Forget that! One of the main objectives of situation tags is to allow you to quickly remember and act on the fact that your response in any situation can be tempered by the myriad possibilities that arise because of education, experience, planning, and, hopefully, caring and compassion. "Equal and opposite" almost always results in "lose-lose"; you will be injured as much as you injure me if we butt forehead to forehead.

The tags I have been describing help me avoid "equal and opposite" and instead apply directed, timely, and intelligent intervention. When I encounter a situation similar to one I have tagged, that tag allows me to pull up the folder full of possible responses I have developed specifically to resolve that type of situation. My tags allow me to redirect force toward mutual objectives (the buzz word is *synergy*) rather than reactive and less productive responses. Your own will help you react to situations you tag in the same positive and productive way.

The **Third Law of Motion Denial** Restatement: Rather than reacting in an "equal and opposite" manner, choose to respond with constant intelligent intervention that channels forces in a positive direction.

CONCLUSION

The Lingering Farewell

When we would discuss situation tagging, Richard, the mentor I mentioned at the beginning of this book, would occasionally say, "We ought to write a book about this." When, during meetings or discussions, I have said out loud, "This is a (whatever tag) situation," and proceeded to quickly define and effectively resolve issues based on that tag, others have demanded to know what in the world I was talking about. After I describe situation tagging, as my mentor once did to me, I have often heard, "Wow, you ought to write a book about that." Well, here you have it. I hope you think differently now than you did a few hours or days ago when you started. The system is simple: recognize that situations reoccur; create a thoughtful context for them; tag them with a memorable metaphor, analogy, or aphorism; and the next time a tagged situation occurs, recognize it for what it is and let what you have learned, experienced, and done to resolve issues related to that tag in the past resurface to allow you to respond effectively.

Each of the thirty essays you have read describes one of my most used situation tags, its source, and applications. I outline the issues or questions that they force me to think through as the related situations arise. I have also restated each in the form of a declaration or question. What I typically didn't try to tell you is how I responded to the situations I recognize. (An exception is **Darley's Law**, where I describe solutions for a frustrated Board of Education that was trying to figure out how to reward teachers without activating the consequences described in that tag.) Response varies widely depending on circumstances. I can promise you, however, that knowing the question is a large part of the answer.

Now, a couple of additional tagging hints before we conclude. One, the degree to which a tag is meaningful may depend on which side of the situation you are on, and tags become most useful when you create a context that helps you recall all sides. The **360-Degree Temptation**, for example, relates to stupid rules. However, it should remind us both how to respond to stupid rules as well as how to avoid making stupid rules ourselves. We may be the target or the creator of almost any of the situations discussed, the actor or the acted upon.

Two, now that you're done what do you remember? This book will become most useful and rewarding if you go back and reread one or two essays a day and see how they sit with you, what experience or education they bring to mind, and how you might adjust and rename them to make them your own.

Three, I will be pleased and flattered if in the near future I overhear someone say, "Well, there's a **360-Degree Temptation**!" or "I just decided that one deserved the **Bastogne Response**." I will know someone read my book. But I may also have failed in part of my purpose. While I would certainly be pleased if you adopt my tags, I hope you are motivated to thoughtfully develop your own so you will know what *you* know, use what *you* have learned, and be more effective at recognizing and solving the problems that are part of *your* life.

I leave you with a bonus tag, borrowed from Wilma Dykeman, a favorite author. She uses the tag "Lingering Farewell" to describe the situation where a participant at a social gathering or a meeting looks at her watch and says," My, it's late. I have to leave," and then, having destroyed the ambiance of the gathering and the group's effectiveness, hangs around for another half an hour.

The **Lingering Farewell** Restatement: When you "have to leave," go. When you are done, quit. Good-bye, good luck, and good tagging.

Afterword—a Note from the Field

A few months ago I started a new job, again in an international environment but different from those I had worked in before. It gave me a great opportunity to test whether I really knew how to use past learning and experience in a new setting. In short, do the principles that I present in this book really work?

On the second day I pulled an ax from the ceiling—an employee-benefit problem that had plagued an employer for years. The need to change a problematic rule with minimal ruffling of feathers has called on all my experience with the **Sergeant York Strategy**. Anytime one is in a new place or position, of course, the **Rikki-Tikki-Tavi Imperative** kicks in, and decisions have to be made about where and how to "run and find out." I am in an environment where corruption is rampant and bureaucracy is ponderous. The **Chinese Water Torture** and its corollary against the **Dead Presidents** kick in. Those factors also bring the **Bastogne Response** into frequent use. Potential distractions from all that is new and interesting here raise the **Rhett Retort** time and time again. Infinite demand on limited resources calls upon the **Oliver Twist**, and so on and so on.

With all that is new and demanding, I respond based on what I know I know. Without meaning to sound immodest, I note that folks around me are still expressing surprise that I have learned so quickly and that I can get to the point so fast that they have to hurry to keep up. Why? I have been there before and I know where I am. "This has all happened before, and it will all happen again, but this time…" it is happening to me, here and now, and I am ready.